MznLnx

Missing Links Exam Preps

Exam Prep for

Strategic Management Competitiveness and Globalization

Hitt, Ireland, Hoskisson, 6th Edition

The MznLnx Exam Prep is your link from the texbook and lecture to your exams.
The MznLnx Exam Preps are unauthorized and comprehensive reviews of your textbooks.

All material provided by MznLnx and Rico Publications (c) 2010
Textbook publishers and textbook authors do not particpate in or contribute to these reviews.

MznLnx

Rico Publications

Exam Prep for Strategic Management Competitiveness and Globalization
6th Edition
Hitt, Ireland, Hoskisson

Publisher: Raymond Houge
Assistant Editor: Michael Rouger
Text and Cover Designer: Lisa Buckner
Marketing Manager: Sara Swagger
Project Manager, Editorial Production: Jerry Emerson
Art Director: Vernon Lowerui

Product Manager: Dave Mason
Editorial Assitant: Rachel Guzmanji
Pedagogy: Debra Long
Cover Image: Jim Reed/Getty Images
Text and Cover Printer: City Printing, Inc.
Compositor: Media Mix, Inc.

(c) 2010 Rico Publications
ALL RIGHTS RESERVED. No part of this work covered by the copyright may be reproduced or used in any form or by an means--graphic, electronic, or mechanical, including photocopying, recording, taping, Web distribution, information storage, and retrieval systems, or in any other manner--without the written permission of the publisher.

For more information about our products, contact us at:
Dave.Mason@RicoPublications.com

For permission to use material from this text or product, submit a request online to:
Dave.Mason@RicoPublications.com

Printed in the United States
ISBN:

Contents

CHAPTER 1
Strategic Management and Strategic Competitiveness — 1

CHAPTER 2
The External Environment: Opportunities, Threats, Industry Competition — 13

CHAPTER 3
The Internal Environment: Resources, Capabilities, and Core Competencies — 27

CHAPTER 4
Business-Level Strategy — 36

CHAPTER 5
Competitive Rivalry and Competitive Dynamics — 46

CHAPTER 6
Corporate-Level Strategy — 50

CHAPTER 7
Acquisition and Restructuring Strategies — 63

CHAPTER 8
International Strategy — 73

CHAPTER 9
Cooperative Strategy — 83

CHAPTER 10
Corporate Governance — 92

CHAPTER 11
Organizational Structure and Controls — 105

CHAPTER 12
Strategic Leadership — 110

CHAPTER 13
Strategic Entrepreneurship — 122

ANSWER KEY — 127

TO THE STUDENT

COMPREHENSIVE

The *MznLnx* Exam Prep series is designed to help you pass your exams. Editors at MznLnx review your textbooks and then prepare these practice exams to help you master the textbook material. Unlike study guides, workbooks, and practice tests provided by the texbook publisher and textbook authors, *MznLnx* gives you **all** of the material in each chapter in exam form, not just samples, so you can be sure to nail your exam.

MECHANICAL

The MznLnx Exam Prep series creates exams that will help you learn the subject matter as well as test you on your understanding. Each question is designed to help you master the concept. Just working through the exams, you gain an understanding of the subject--its a simple mechanical process that produces success.

INTEGRATED STUDY GUIDE AND REVIEW

MznLnx is not just a set of exams designed to test you, its also a comprehensive review of the subject content. Each exam question is also a review of the concept, making sure that you will get the answer correct without having to go to other sources of material. You learn as you go! Its the easiest way to pass an exam.

HUMOR

Studying can be tedious and dry. MznLnx's instructional design includes moderate humor within the exam questions on occassion, to break the tedium and revitalize the brain

Chapter 1. Strategic Management and Strategic Competitiveness

1. The phrase mergers and _____s refers to the aspect of corporate strategy, corporate finance and management dealing with the buying, selling and combining of different companies that can aid, finance, or help a growing company in a given industry grow rapidly without having to create another business entity.

    An _____, also known as a takeover or a buyout, is the buying of one company (the 'target') by another. An _____ may be friendly or hostile.

    a. A Stake in the Outcome
    b. A4e
    c. Acquisition
    d. AAAI

2. _____ is, in very basic words, a position a firm occupies against its competitors.

    According to Michael Porter, the three methods for creating a sustainable _____ are through:

    1. Cost leadership

    2. Differentiation

    3. Focus (economics)

    a. Competitive advantage
    b. 1990 Clean Air Act
    c. 28-hour day
    d. Theory Z

3. In decision theory and estimation theory, the _____ of an estimator, $\hat{\theta}$, of an unknown parameter of the distribution, θ, is the expected value of the loss function

$$R(\theta, \hat{\theta}) = \mathbb{E}_\theta L(\theta, \hat{\theta}) = \int L(\theta, \hat{\theta}) \, dP_\theta.$$

Chapter 1. Strategic Management and Strategic Competitiveness

where dP_θ is a probability measure parametrized by θ.

- For a scalar parameter θ and a quadratic loss function,

$$L(\theta, \hat{\theta}) = (\theta - \hat{\theta})^2$$

the _____ function becomes the mean squared error of the estimate,

$$R(\theta, \hat{\theta}) = E_\theta (\theta - \hat{\theta})^2$$

- In density estimation, the unknown parameter is probability density itself. The loss function is typically chosen to be a norm in an appropriate function space. For example, for L^2 norm,

$$L(f, \hat{f}) = \|f - \hat{f}\|_2^2$$

the _____ function becomes the mean integrated squared error

$$R(f, \hat{f}) = E\|f - \hat{f}\|^2$$

a. Risk
b. Linear model
c. Risk aversion
d. Financial modeling

4. _____ is a process of planning and controlling the performance or execution of any type of activity, such as:

- a project (project _____) or
- a process (process _____, sometimes referred to as the process performance measurement and management system.)

Organization's senior management is responsible for carrying out its _____.

a. Management process
b. Participatory management
c. Work design
d. Human Relations Movement

Chapter 1. Strategic Management and Strategic Competitiveness

5. _____ is a legally declared inability or impairment of ability of an individual or organization to pay its creditors. Creditors may file a _____ petition against a debtor ('involuntary _____') in an effort to recoup a portion of what they are owed or initiate a restructuring. In the majority of cases, however, _____ is initiated by the debtor (a 'voluntary _____' that is filed by the insolvent individual or organization.)
   a. Bankruptcy
   b. 28-hour day
   c. 33 Strategies of War
   d. 1990 Clean Air Act

6. _____ is a business magazine published by McGraw-Hill. It was first published in 1929 (as The Business Week) under the direction of Malcolm Muir, who was serving as president of the McGraw-Hill Publishing company at the time. Its primary competitors in the national business magazine category are Fortune and Forbes, which are published bi-weekly.
   a. BusinessWeek
   b. Democracy in America
   c. Hotel Vikas
   d. The Wealth of Nations

7. Often a characteristic of new markets and industries, _____ occurs when technologies or offerings are so new that standards and rules are in flux, resulting in competitive advantages that cannot be sustained. In response, companies must constantly compete in price or quality, or innovate in supply chain management, new value creation, or have enough financial capital to outlast other competitors.
   a. Learning-by-doing
   b. Hypercompetition
   c. NAIRU
   d. Dominant Design

8. _____ is a broad label that refers to any individuals or households that use goods and services generated within the economy. The concept of a _____ is used in different contexts, so that the usage and significance of the term may vary.

   Typically when business people and economists talk of _____s they are talking about person as _____, an aggregated commodity item with little individuality other than that expressed in the buy/not-buy decision.

   a. Consumer
   b. 28-hour day
   c. 1990 Clean Air Act
   d. 33 Strategies of War

9. _____ according to Onuoha (2007) is the practice of starting new organizations or revitalizing mature organizations, particularly new businesses generally in response to identified opportunities. _____ is often a difficult undertaking, as a vast majority of new businesses fail. Entrepreneurial activities are substantially different depending on the type of organization that is being started.
   a. AAAI
   b. A4e
   c. A Stake in the Outcome
   d. Entrepreneurship

10. _____ is exchange of capital, goods, and services across international borders or territories. In most countries, it represents a significant share of gross domestic product (GDP.) While _____ has been present throughout much of history , its economic, social, and political importance has been on the rise in recent centuries.
   a. International trade
   b. A4e
   c. AAAI
   d. A Stake in the Outcome

11. The _____ or gross domestic income (GDI), a basic measure of an economy's economic performance, is the market value of all final goods and services made within the borders of a nation in a year. _____ can be defined in three ways, all of which are conceptually identical. First, it is equal to the total expenditures for all final goods and services produced within the country in a stipulated period of time (usually a 365-day year).
   a. Productivity management
   b. Human capital
   c. Gross domestic product
   d. Perfect competition

12. _____ is the branch of economics that studies the dynamics of exchange rates, foreign investment, and how these affect international trade. It also studies international projects, international investments and capital flows, and trade deficits. It includes the study of futures, options and currency swaps.
   a. AAAI
   b. A Stake in the Outcome
   c. A4e
   d. International finance

13. _____ in its literal sense is the process of transformation of local or regional phenomena into global ones. It can be described as a process by which the people of the world are unified into a single society and function together.

This process is a combination of economic, technological, sociocultural and political forces.

a. Cost Management
b. Collaborative Planning, Forecasting and Replenishment
c. Globalization
d. Histogram

14. A _____ is a business that is privately owned and operated, with a small number of employees and relatively low volume of sales. The legal definition of 'small' often varies by country and industry, but is generally under 100 employees in the United States and under 50 employees in the European Union. In comparison, the definition of mid-sized business by the number of employees is generally under 500 in the U.S. and 250 for the European Union.
    a. Golden Boot Compensation
    b. Small business
    c. Critical Success Factor
    d. Pre-determined overhead rate

15. _____ is the process by which a new idea or new product is accepted by the market. The rate of _____ is the speed that the new idea spreads from one consumer to the next. Adoption is similar to _____ except that it deals with the psychological processes an individual goes through, rather than an aggregate market process.
    a. Mass marketing
    b. Value chain
    c. Category management
    d. Diffusion

16. _____, commonly known as e-commerce, consists of the buying and selling of products or services over electronic systems such as the Internet and other computer networks. The amount of trade conducted electronically has grown extraordinarily with widespread Internet usage. The use of commerce is conducted in this way, spurring and drawing on innovations in electronic funds transfer, supply chain management, Internet marketing, online transaction processing, electronic data interchange (EDI), inventory management systems, and automated data collection systems.
    a. A4e
    b. Online shopping
    c. Electronic Commerce
    d. A Stake in the Outcome

17. A _____ is a set of exclusive rights granted by a state to an inventor or his assignee for a limited period of time in exchange for a disclosure of an invention.

The procedure for granting _____s, the requirements placed on the _____ee and the extent of the exclusive rights vary widely between countries according to national laws and international agreements. Typically, however, a _____ application must include one or more claims defining the invention which must be new, inventive, and useful or industrially applicable.

a. Food, Drug, and Cosmetic Act
b. Labor Management Reporting and Disclosure Act
c. Federal Trade Commission Act
d. Patent

18. _____ refers to metrics and measures of output from production processes, per unit of input. Labor _____, for example, is typically measured as a ratio of output per labor-hour, an input. _____ may be conceived of as a metrics of the technical or engineering efficiency of production.
a. Value engineering
b. Master production schedule
c. Remanufacturing
d. Productivity

19. A chief executive officer (_____) or chief executive is one of the highest-ranking corporate officer (executive) or administrator in charge of total management. An individual selected as President and _____ of a corporation, company, organization, or agency, reports to the board of directors. In internal communication and press releases, many companies capitalize the term and those of other high positions, even when they are not proper nouns.
a. Portfolio manager
b. Director of communications
c. Chief executive officer
d. CEO

20. _____ are defined as identifiable non-monetary assets that cannot be seen, touched or physically measured, which are created through time and/or effort and that are identifiable as a separate asset. There are two primary forms of intangibles - legal intangibles (such as trade secrets (e.g., customer lists), copyrights, patents, trademarks, and goodwill) and competitive intangibles (such as knowledge activities (know-how, knowledge), collaboration activities, leverage activities, and structural activities.) Legal intangibles are known under the generic term intellectual property and generate legal property rights defensible in a court of law.
a. Intangible assets
b. Interlocking directorate
c. Induction programme
d. Employee value proposition

Chapter 1. Strategic Management and Strategic Competitiveness

21. In business and accounting, _____s are everything of value that is owned by a person or company. Any property or object of value that one possesses, usually considered as applicable to the payment of one's debts is considered an _____. Simplistically stated, _____s are things of value that can be readily converted into cash.

a. A4e
b. A Stake in the Outcome
c. AAAI
d. Asset

22. A _____ is a special kind of database for knowledge management, providing the means for the computerized collection, organization, and retrieval of knowledge.

_____s are categorized into two major types:

- Machine-readable _____s store knowledge in a computer-readable form, usually for the purpose of having automated deductive reasoning applied to them. They contain a set of data, often in the form of rules that describe the knowledge in a logically consistent manner. An ontology can define the structure of stored data - what types of entities are recorded and what their relationships are. Logical operators, such as And (conjunction), Or (disjunction), material implication and negation may be used to build it up from simpler pieces of information. Consequently, classical deduction can be used to reason about the knowledge in the _____. Some machine-readable _____s are used with artificial intelligence, for example as part of an expert system that focuses on a domain like prescription drugs or customs law. Such _____s are also used by the semantic web.

- Human-readable _____s are designed to allow people to retrieve and use the knowledge they contain. They are commonly used to complement a help desk or for sharing information among employees within an organization. They might store troubleshooting information, articles, white papers, user manuals, or answers to frequently asked questions.

a. 1990 Clean Air Act
b. Knowledge base
c. 33 Strategies of War
d. 28-hour day

23. _____ is something that a firm can do well and that meets the following three conditions:

Competencies are things that companys execute well across several business units or product sectors.

Firms usually have few competencies, but these are usually less liable to change rapidly.

1. It provides consumer benefits
2. It is not easy for competitors to imitate
3. It can be leveraged widely to many products and markets.

A _____ can take various forms, including technical/subject matter know-how, a reliable process and/or close relationships with customers and suppliers (Mascarenhas et al. 1998.)

a. Core competency
b. Dominant Design
c. Learning-by-doing
d. NAIRU

24. _____ is an advertisement in which a particular product specifically mentions a competitor by name for the express purpose of showing why the competitor is inferior to the product naming it.

This should not be confused with parody advertisements, where a fictional product is being advertised for the purpose of poking fun at the particular advertisement, nor should it be confused with the use of a coined brand name for the purpose of comparing the product without actually naming an actual competitor. ('Wikipedia tastes better and is less filling than the Encyclopedia Galactica.')

In the 1980s, during what has been referred to as the cola wars, soft-drink manufacturer Pepsi ran a series of advertisements where people, caught on hidden camera, in a blind taste test, chose Pepsi over rival Coca-Cola.

a. 28-hour day
b. 33 Strategies of War
c. 1990 Clean Air Act
d. Comparative advertising

25. A mutual _____ or stockholder is an individual or company (including a corporation) that legally owns one or more shares of stock in a joint stock company. A company's _____s collectively own that company. Thus, the typical goal of such companies is to enhance _____ value.
a. Stockholder
b. Free riding
c. Shareholder
d. 1990 Clean Air Act

Chapter 1. Strategic Management and Strategic Competitiveness

26. _____ is a concept related to the relative abilities of parties in a situation to exert influence over each other. If both parties are on an equal footing in a debate, then they will have equal _____, such as in a perfectly competitive market, or between an evenly matched monopoly and monopsony.

There are a number of fields where the concept of _____ has proven crucial to coherent analysis: game theory, labour economics, collective bargaining arrangements, diplomatic negotiations, settlement of litigation, the price of insurance, and any negotiation in general.

a. Trade credit
b. 1990 Clean Air Act
c. Buy-sell agreement
d. Bargaining power

27. _____ has been described as the 'process of social influence in which one person can enlist the aid and support of others in the accomplishment of a common task' . A definition more inclusive of followers comes from Alan Keith of Genentech who said '_____ is ultimately about creating a way for people to contribute to making something extraordinary happen.'

_____ is one of the most salient aspects of the organizational context. However, defining _____ has been challenging.

a. Leadership
b. Situational leadership
c. 28-hour day
d. 1990 Clean Air Act

28. _____ is an idea in the field of Organizational studies and management which describes the psychology, attitudes, experiences, beliefs and Values (personal and cultural values) of an organization. It has been defined as 'the specific collection of values and norms that are shared by people and groups in an organization and that control the way they interact with each other and with stakeholders outside the organization.'

This definition continues to explain organizational values also known as 'beliefs and ideas about what kinds of goals members of an organization should pursue and ideas about the appropriate kinds or standards of behavior organizational members should use to achieve these goals. From organizational values develop organizational norms, guidelines or expectations that prescribe appropriate kinds of behavior by employees in particular situations and control the behavior of organizational members towards one another.'

_____ is not the same as corporate culture.

a. Union shop
b. Organizational development
c. Organizational effectiveness
d. Organizational culture

29. _____ can be regarded as an outcome of mental processes (cognitive process) leading to the selection of a course of action among several alternatives. Every _____ process produces a final choice. The output can be an action or an opinion of choice.
   a. 33 Strategies of War
   b. Decision making
   c. 1990 Clean Air Act
   d. 28-hour day

30. In game theory, an _____ is a set of moves or strategies taken by the players, or their payoffs resulting from the actions or strategies taken by all players. The two are complementary in that given knowledge of the set of strategies of all players, the final state of the game is known, as are any relevant payoffs. In a game where chance or a random event is involved, the _____ is not known from only the set of strategies, but is only realized when the random event(s) are realized.
   a. Outcome
   b. A4e
   c. AAAI
   d. A Stake in the Outcome

31. _____ Management is the succession of strategies used by management as a product goes through its _____. The conditions in which a product is sold changes over time and must be managed as it moves through its succession of stages.

The _____ goes through many phases, involves many professional disciplines, and requires many skills, tools and processes.

   a. Golden handshake
   b. Job hunting
   c. Product life cycle
   d. Strategic Alliance

Chapter 1. Strategic Management and Strategic Competitiveness   11

32. In economics, _____ is a measure of the relative satisfaction from consumption of various goods and services. Given this measure, one may speak meaningfully of increasing or decreasing _____, and thereby explain economic behavior in terms of attempts to increase one's _____. For illustrative purposes, changes in _____ are sometimes expressed in units called utils.

   a. A Stake in the Outcome
   b. Ordinal utility
   c. Utility
   d. Indirect utility function

33. _____ is the ethics of an organization, and it is how an organization ethically responds to an internal or external stimulus. _____ is interdependent with the organizational culture. Although, it is akin to both organizational behavior (OB) and business ethics on the micro and macro levels, _____ is neither OB, nor is it solely business ethics (which includes corporate governance and corporate ethics.)

   a. A Stake in the Outcome
   b. A4e
   c. AAAI
   d. Organizational ethics

34. A _____ is a brief written statement of the purpose of a company or organization. Ideally, a _____ guides the actions of the organization, spells out its overall goal, provides a sense of direction, and guides decision making for all levels of management.

_____s often contain the following:

- Purpose and aim of the organization
- The organization's primary stakeholders: clients, stockholders, etc.
- Responsibilities of the organization toward these stakeholders
- Products and services offered

In developing a _____:

- Encourage as much input as feasible from employees, volunteers, and other stakeholders
- Publicize it broadly

The _____ can be used to resolve differences between business stakeholders. Stakeholders include: employees including managers and executives, stockholders, board of directors, customers, suppliers, distributors, creditors, governments (local, state, federal, etc.), unions, competitors, NGO's, and the general public.

a. 33 Strategies of War
b. 1990 Clean Air Act
c. 28-hour day
d. Mission statement

Chapter 2. The External Environment: Opportunities, Threats, Industry Competition

1. In economics, _____ is the desire to own something and the ability to pay for it. The term _____ signifies the ability or the willingness to buy a particular commodity at a given point of time.
   a. 28-hour day
   b. 33 Strategies of War
   c. 1990 Clean Air Act
   d. Demand

2. _____ is the branch of economics that studies the dynamics of exchange rates, foreign investment, and how these affect international trade. It also studies international projects, international investments and capital flows, and trade deficits. It includes the study of futures, options and currency swaps.
   a. A Stake in the Outcome
   b. AAAI
   c. A4e
   d. International finance

3. _____ or _____ data refers to selected population characteristics as used in government, marketing or opinion research, or the _____ profiles used in such research. Note the distinction from the term 'demography' Commonly-used _____s include race, age, income, disabilities, mobility (in terms of travel time to work or number of vehicles available), educational attainment, home ownership, employment status, and even location.
   a. Abraham Harold Maslow
   b. Adam Smith
   c. Demographic
   d. Affiliation

4. _____ in marketing and strategic management is an assessment of the strengths and weaknesses of current and potential competitors. This analysis provides both an offensive and defensive strategic context through which to identify opportunities and threats. Competitor profiling coalesces all of the relevant sources of _____ into one framework in the support of efficient and effective strategy formulation, implementation, monitoring and adjustment.
   a. 1990 Clean Air Act
   b. 28-hour day
   c. Competitor or Competitive Intelligence
   d. Competitor analysis

5. In general, a _____ is an arrangement to provide people with an income when they are no longer earning a regular income from employment.

The terms retirement plan or superannuation refer to a _____ granted upon retirement . Retirement plans may be set up by employers, insurance companies, the government or other institutions such as employer associations or trade unions.

a. Pension
b. Wage
c. State Compensation Insurance Fund
d. Pension insurance contract

6. _____ is the point where a person stops employment completely. A person may also semi-retire and keep some sort of _____ job, out of choice rather than necessity. This usually happens upon reaching a determined age, when physical conditions don't allow the person to work any more (by illness or accident), or even for personal choice (usually in the presence of an adequate pension or personal savings.)
   a. Termination of employment
   b. Severance package
   c. Wrongful dismissal
   d. Retirement

7. _____ is an advertisement in which a particular product specifically mentions a competitor by name for the express purpose of showing why the competitor is inferior to the product naming it.

This should not be confused with parody advertisements, where a fictional product is being advertised for the purpose of poking fun at the particular advertisement, nor should it be confused with the use of a coined brand name for the purpose of comparing the product without actually naming an actual competitor. ('Wikipedia tastes better and is less filling than the Encyclopedia Galactica.')

In the 1980s, during what has been referred to as the cola wars, soft-drink manufacturer Pepsi ran a series of advertisements where people, caught on hidden camera, in a blind taste test, chose Pepsi over rival Coca-Cola.

   a. Comparative advertising
   b. 1990 Clean Air Act
   c. 33 Strategies of War
   d. 28-hour day

8. _____ is the process of estimation in unknown situations. Prediction is a similar, but more general term. Both can refer to estimation of time series, cross-sectional or longitudinal data.
   a. 1990 Clean Air Act
   b. 28-hour day
   c. Forecasting
   d. 33 Strategies of War

Chapter 2. The External Environment: Opportunities, Threats, Industry Competition

9. _____ refers to the methods of practicing and using another person's business philosophy. The franchisor grants the independent operator the right to distribute its products, techniques, and trademarks for a percentage of gross monthly sales and a royalty fee. Various tangibles and intangibles such as national or international advertising, training, and other support services are commonly made available by the franchisor.

a. 28-hour day
b. 1990 Clean Air Act
c. Franchising
d. ServiceMaster

10. The _____ or gross domestic income (GDI), a basic measure of an economy's economic performance, is the market value of all final goods and services made within the borders of a nation in a year. _____ can be defined in three ways, all of which are conceptually identical. First, it is equal to the total expenditures for all final goods and services produced within the country in a stipulated period of time (usually a 365-day year).

a. Human capital
b. Perfect competition
c. Gross domestic product
d. Productivity management

11. The _____ is the labour pool in employment. It is generally used to describe those working for a single company or industry, but can also apply to a geographic region like a city, country, state, etc. The term generally excludes the employers or management, and implies those involved in manual labour.

a. Workforce
b. Division of labour
c. Work-life balance
d. Pink-collar worker

12. _____ is one of the four elements of marketing mix. An organization or set of organizations (go-betweens) involved in the process of making a product or service available for use or consumption by a consumer or business user.

The other three parts of the marketing mix are product, pricing, and promotion.

a. Missing completely at random
b. Job creation programs
c. Matching theory
d. Distribution

Chapter 2. The External Environment: Opportunities, Threats, Industry Competition

13. The 'business case for _____', theorizes that in a global marketplace, a company that employs a diverse workforce (both men and women, people of many generations, people from ethnically and racially diverse backgrounds etc.) is better able to understand the demographics of the marketplace it serves and is thus better equipped to thrive in that marketplace than a company that has a more limited range of employee demographics.

An additional corollary suggests that a company that supports the _____ of its workforce can also improve employee satisfaction, productivity and retention.

   a. Trademark
   b. Virtual team
   c. Diversity
   d. Kanban

14. _____ is the incidence or process of transferring ownership of a business, enterprise, agency or public service from the public sector (government) to the private sector (business.) In a broader sense, _____ refers to transfer of any government function to the private sector including governmental functions like revenue collection and law enforcement.
   a. 28-hour day
   b. 1990 Clean Air Act
   c. Performance reports
   d. Privatization

15. A _____ is a general term that describes any government policy or regulation that restricts international trade. The barriers can take many forms, including the following terms that include many restrictions in international trade within multiple countries that import and export any items of trade.

   - Import duty
   - Import licenses
   - Export licenses
   - Import quotas
   - Tariffs
   - Subsidies
   - Non-tariff barriers to trade
   - Voluntary Export Restraints
   - Local Content Requirements
   - Embargo

Most _____s work on the same principle: the imposition of some sort of cost on trade that raises the price of the traded products. If two or more nations repeatedly use _____s against each other, then a trade war results.

a. Customs brokerage
b. Most favoured nation
c. Trade creation
d. Trade barrier

16. _____ is a form of communication that typically attempts to persuade potential customers to purchase or to consume more of a particular brand of product or service. 'While now central to the contemporary global economy and the reproduction of global production networks, it is only quite recently that _____ has been more than a marginal influence on patterns of sales and production. The formation of modern _____ was intimately bound up with the emergence of new forms of monopoly capitalism around the end of the 19th and beginning of the 20th century as one element in corporate strategies to create, organize and where possible control markets, especially for mass produced consumer goods.

a. A4e
b. AAAI
c. Advertising
d. A Stake in the Outcome

17. The _____ is an agency of the United States Department of Health and Human Services and is responsible for regulating and supervising the safety of foods, dietary supplements, drugs, vaccines, biological medical products, blood products, medical devices, radiation-emitting devices, veterinary products, and cosmetics. The FDA also enforces section 361 of the Public Health Service Act and the associated regulations, including sanitation requirements on interstate travel as well as specific rules for control of disease on products ranging from pet turtles to semen donations for assisted reproductive medicine techniques.

The FDA is an agency within the United States Department of Health and Human Services responsible for protecting and promoting the nation's public health.

a. 33 Strategies of War
b. 28-hour day
c. 1990 Clean Air Act
d. Food and Drug Administration

18. _____ is a type of trade policy that allows traders to act and transact without interference from government. Thus, the policy permits trading partners mutual gains from trade, with goods and services produced according to the theory of comparative advantage.

Under a _____ policy, prices are a reflection of true supply and demand, and are the sole determinant of resource allocation.

a. Free trade
b. 33 Strategies of War
c. 1990 Clean Air Act
d. 28-hour day

19. The _____ is a trilateral trade bloc in North America created by the governments of the United States, Canada, and Mexico. The agreement creating the trade bloc came into force on January 1, 1994. It superseded the Canada-United States Free Trade Agreement between the U.S. and Canada.
a. Business war game
b. Trade union
c. Career portfolios
d. North American Free Trade Agreement

20. The _____, sometimes called the Puritan Work Ethic, is a sociological, theoretical concept. It is based upon the notion that the Calvinist emphasis on the necessity for hard work is proponent of a person's calling and worldly success is a sign of personal salvation. It is argued that Protestants beginning with Martin Luther had reconceptualised worldly work as a duty which benefits both the individual and society as a whole.
a. 33 Strategies of War
b. 28-hour day
c. 1990 Clean Air Act
d. Protestant work ethic

21. _____ is a set of values based on hard work and diligence. It is also a belief in the moral benefit of work and its ability to enhance character. An example would be the Protestant _____.
a. 1990 Clean Air Act
b. 33 Strategies of War
c. Work ethic
d. 28-hour day

22. The phrase mergers and _____s refers to the aspect of corporate strategy, corporate finance and management dealing with the buying, selling and combining of different companies that can aid, finance, or help a growing company in a given industry grow rapidly without having to create another business entity.

An _____, also known as a takeover or a buyout, is the buying of one company (the 'target') by another. An _____ may be friendly or hostile.

a. AAAI
b. A4e
c. A Stake in the Outcome
d. Acquisition

23. _____, e-commuting, e-work, telework, working from home (WFH), or working at home (WAH) is a work arrangement in which employees enjoy flexibility in working location and hours. In other words, the daily commute to a central place of work is replaced by telecommunication links. Many work from home, while others, occasionally also referred to as nomad workers or web commuters utilize mobile telecommunications technology to work from coffee shops or myriad other locations.
   a. 1990 Clean Air Act
   b. 33 Strategies of War
   c. 28-hour day
   d. Telecommuting

24. _____ in its literal sense is the process of transformation of local or regional phenomena into global ones. It can be described as a process by which the people of the world are unified into a single society and function together.

This process is a combination of economic, technological, sociocultural and political forces.

   a. Collaborative Planning, Forecasting and Replenishment
   b. Histogram
   c. Cost Management
   d. Globalization

25. In economics, business, retail, and accounting, a _____ is the value of money that has been used up to produce something, and hence is not available for use anymore. In economics, a _____ is an alternative that is given up as a result of a decision. In business, the _____ may be one of acquisition, in which case the amount of money expended to acquire it is counted as _____.
   a. Cost
   b. Cost allocation
   c. Cost overrun
   d. Fixed costs

26. _____ is subcontracting a process, such as product design or manufacturing, to a third-party company. The decision to outsource is often made in the interest of lowering cost or making better use of time and energy costs, redirecting or conserving energy directed at the competencies of a particular business, or to make more efficient use of land, labor, capital, (information) technology and resources. _____ became part of the business lexicon during the 1980s.

Chapter 2. The External Environment: Opportunities, Threats, Industry Competition

a. Outsourcing
b. Opinion leadership
c. Unemployment insurance
d. Operant conditioning

27. _____ refers to the stock of skills and knowledge embodied in the ability to perform labor so as to produce economic value. It is the skills and knowledge gained by a worker through education and experience. Many early economic theories refer to it simply as labor, one of three factors of production, and consider it to be a fungible resource -- homogeneous and easily interchangeable.

a. Human capital
b. Deflation
c. Market structure
d. Productivity management

28. The loyalty business model is a business model used in strategic management in which company resources are employed so as to increase the loyalty of customers and other stakeholders in the expectation that corporate objectives will be met or surpassed. A typical example of this type of model is: quality of product or service leads to customer satisfaction, which leads to _____, which leads to profitability.

Fredrick Reichheld (1996) expanded the loyalty business model beyond customers and employees.

a. 33 Strategies of War
b. 28-hour day
c. 1990 Clean Air Act
d. Customer loyalty

29. _____, in microeconomics, are the cost advantages that a business obtains due to expansion. They are factors that cause a producer's average cost per unit to fall as scale is increased. _____ is a long run concept and refers to reductions in unit cost as the size of a facility, or scale, increases.

a. A4e
b. Economies of scope
c. Economies of scale
d. A Stake in the Outcome

30. A _____ system is a manufacturing system in which there is some amount of flexibility that allows the system to react in the case of changes, whether predicted or unpredicted. This flexibility is generally considered to fall into two categories, which both contain numerous subcategories.

Chapter 2. The External Environment: Opportunities, Threats, Industry Competition

The first category, machine flexibility, covers the system's ability to be changed to produce new product types, and ability to change the order of operations executed on a part. The second category is called routing flexibility, which consists of the ability to use multiple machines to perform the same operation on a part, as well as the system's ability to absorb large-scale changes, such as in volume, capacity, or capability.

a. Jidoka
b. Flexible manufacturing
c. Manufacturing resource planning
d. Homeworkers

31. _____, in marketing, manufacturing, call centres and management, is the use of flexible computer-aided manufacturing systems to produce custom output. Those systems combine the low unit costs of mass production processes with the flexibility of individual customization.

'_____' is the new frontier in business competition for both manufacturing and service industries.

a. 28-hour day
b. 33 Strategies of War
c. 1990 Clean Air Act
d. Mass customization

32. In marketing, _____ is the process of distinguishing the differences of a product or offering from others, to make it more attractive to a particular target market. This involves differentiating it from competitors' products as well as one's own product offerings.
a. Product differentiation
b. Market share
c. Market development
d. PEST analysis

33. Network externalities resemble economies of scale, but they are not considered such because they are a function of the number of users of a good or service in an industry, not of the production efficiency within a business. _____ are only considered examples of network externalities if they are driven by demand side economies.

Chapter 2. The External Environment: Opportunities, Threats, Industry Competition

Formally, a production function $F(K,L)$ is defined to have:

- constant returns to scale if (for any constant a greater than or equal to 0) $F(aK, aL) = aF(K,L)$
- increasing returns to scale if (for any constant a greater than 1) $F(aK, aL) > aF(K,L)$
- decreasing returns to scale if (for any constant a greater than 1) $F(aK, aL) < aF(K,L)$

where K and L are factors of production, capital and labour, respectively.

As an example, the Cobb-Douglas functional form has constant returns to scale when the sum of the exponents adds up to one.

a. A4e
b. A Stake in the Outcome
c. AAAI
d. Economies of scale external to the firm

34. In economics and especially in the theory of competition, _____ are obstacles in the path of a firm that make it difficult to enter a given market.

_____ are the source of a firm's pricing power - the ability of a firm to raise prices without losing all its customers.

The term refers to hindrances that an individual may face while trying to gain entrance into a profession or trade.

a. 1990 Clean Air Act
b. Predatory pricing
c. 28-hour day
d. Barriers to entry

35. The _____ is a bank regulation, which sets a framework on how banks and depository institutions must handle their capital. The categorization of assets and capital is highly standardized so that it can be risk weighted. Internationally, the Basel Committee on Banking Supervision housed at the Bank for International Settlements influence each country's banking _____ s.

a. Reserve requirement
b. 1990 Clean Air Act
c. Lock box
d. Capital requirement

36. _____ is the removal or simplification of government rules and regulations that constrain the operation of market forces. _____ does not mean elimination of laws against fraud, but eliminating or reducing government control of how business is done, thereby moving toward a more free market.

The stated rationale for '_____' is often that fewer and simpler regulations will lead to a raised level of competitiveness, therefore higher productivity, more efficiency and lower prices overall.

a. Value added
b. Deregulation
c. Natural rate of unemployment
d. Rehn-Meidner Model

37. Switching barriers or _____s are terms used in microeconomics, strategic management, and marketing to describe any impediment to a customer's changing of suppliers.

In many markets, consumers are forced to incur costs when switching from one supplier to another. These costs are called _____s and can come in many different shapes.

a. Strategic group
b. Strategic business unit
c. Switching cost
d. Corporate strategy

38. A _____ is typically described as a deliberate plan of action to guide decisions and achieve rational outcome(s.) However, the term may also be used to denote what is actually done, even though it is unplanned.

The term may apply to government, private sector organizations and groups, and individuals.

a. 28-hour day
b. 33 Strategies of War
c. 1990 Clean Air Act
d. Policy

Chapter 2. The External Environment: Opportunities, Threats, Industry Competition

39. _____ is a concept related to the relative abilities of parties in a situation to exert influence over each other. If both parties are on an equal footing in a debate, then they will have equal _____, such as in a perfectly competitive market, or between an evenly matched monopoly and monopsony.

There are a number of fields where the concept of _____ has proven crucial to coherent analysis: game theory, labour economics, collective bargaining arrangements, diplomatic negotiations, settlement of litigation, the price of insurance, and any negotiation in general.

   a. 1990 Clean Air Act
   b. Trade credit
   c. Buy-sell agreement
   d. Bargaining power

40. A niche market is the subset of the market on which a specific product is focusing on; Therefore the _____ defines the specific product features aimed at satisfying specific market needs, as well as the price range, production quality and the demographics that is intended to impact.

Every single product that is on sale can be defined by its niche market. As of special note, the products aimed at a wide demographics audience, with the resulting low price (due to Price elasticity of demand), are said to belong to the Mainstream niche, in practice referred only as Mainstream or of high demand.

   a. Dominant logic
   b. Labor intensive
   c. Prevailing wage
   d. Market niche

41. _____ is a concept developed by Michael Porter, used in business strategy. It describes a way to establish the competitive advantage. _____, in basic words, means the lowest cost of operation in the industry.
   a. Cost leadership
   b. Strategic group
   c. Strategic business unit
   d. Switching cost

42. _____ has been described as the 'process of social influence in which one person can enlist the aid and support of others in the accomplishment of a common task' . A definition more inclusive of followers comes from Alan Keith of Genentech who said '_____ is ultimately about creating a way for people to contribute to making something extraordinary happen.'

_____ is one of the most salient aspects of the organizational context. However, defining _____ has been challenging.

Chapter 2. The External Environment: Opportunities, Threats, Industry Competition

a. Situational leadership
b. 1990 Clean Air Act
c. 28-hour day
d. Leadership

43. _____ is the state or fact of exclusive rights and control over property, which may be an object, land/real estate or intellectual property. An _____ right is also referred to as title. The concept of _____ has existed for thousands of years and in all cultures.
   a. A4e
   b. Emanation of the state
   c. Ownership
   d. A Stake in the Outcome

44. _____ is a concept in economics which refers to the extent to which an enterprise or a nation actually uses its installed productive capacity. Thus, it refers to the relationship between actual output that 'is' produced with the installed equipment and the potential output which 'could' be produced with it, if capacity was fully used.

If market demand grows, _____ will rise.

   a. Multifactor productivity
   b. Diseconomies of scale
   c. Factors of production
   d. Capacity utilization

45. In economics, _____ are business expenses that are not dependent on the activities of the business They tend to be time-related, such as salaries or rents being paid per month. This is in contrast to variable costs, which are volume-related (and are paid per quantity.)

In management accounting, _____ are defined as expenses that do not change in proportion to the activity of a business, within the relevant period or scale of production.

   a. Cost allocation
   b. Fixed costs
   c. Cost of quality
   d. Transaction cost

Chapter 2. The External Environment: Opportunities, Threats, Industry Competition

46. _____ is a term used to define maximum possible output of an economy. According to UNCTAD, no agreed-upon definition exists. UNCTAD itself proposes: 'the productive resources, entrepreneurial capabilities and production linkages which together determine the capacity of a country to produce goods and services.' The term '_____' is also used in binary economics to mean income-generating capacity be it of a factory, land, patent or the labour skills of an individual.
   a. Factors of production
   b. Productive capacity
   c. Diseconomies of scale
   d. Multifactor productivity

47. In economics, _____ are obstacles in the path of a firm which wants to leave a given market or industrial sector. These obstacles often cost the firm financially to leave the market and may prohibit it doing so.

If the barriers of exit are significant; a firm may be forced to continue competing in a market, as the costs of leaving may be higher than those incurred if they continue competing in the market.

   a. 1990 Clean Air Act
   b. 28-hour day
   c. Barriers to exit
   d. 33 Strategies of War

48. A _____ is a concept used in strategic management that groups companies within an industry that have similar business models or similar combinations of strategies. For example, the restaurant industry can be divided into several _____s including fast-food and fine-dining based on variables such as preparation time, pricing, and presentation. The number of groups within an industry and their composition depends on the dimensions used to define the groups.
   a. Strategic group
   b. Corporate strategy
   c. Strategic business unit
   d. Strategic drift

49. _____ is the original form of externally-oriented business intelligence that preceded Knowledge Management or Data Mining as the primary concern of executives responsible for increasing market share.
   a. 28-hour day
   b. Competitor analysis
   c. 1990 Clean Air Act
   d. Competitor or Competitive Intelligence

Chapter 3. The Internal Environment: Resources, Capabilities, and Core Competencies

1. A _____ is a relatively new executive level position at a corporation, company, organization typically reporting directly to the CEO or board of directors. The _____ is responsible for a brand's image, experience, and promise, and propagating it throughout all aspects of the company. The brand officer oversees marketing, advertising, design, public relations and customer service departments.

   a. Purchasing manager
   b. Chief executive officer
   c. Chief brand officer
   d. Director of communications

2. _____ is, in very basic words, a position a firm occupies against its competitors.

According to Michael Porter, the three methods for creating a sustainable _____ are through:

1. Cost leadership

2. Differentiation

3. Focus (economics)

   a. Theory Z
   b. 1990 Clean Air Act
   c. 28-hour day
   d. Competitive advantage

3. _____ is an advertisement in which a particular product specifically mentions a competitor by name for the express purpose of showing why the competitor is inferior to the product naming it.

This should not be confused with parody advertisements, where a fictional product is being advertised for the purpose of poking fun at the particular advertisement, nor should it be confused with the use of a coined brand name for the purpose of comparing the product without actually naming an actual competitor. ('Wikipedia tastes better and is less filling than the Encyclopedia Galactica.')

In the 1980s, during what has been referred to as the cola wars, soft-drink manufacturer Pepsi ran a series of advertisements where people, caught on hidden camera, in a blind taste test, chose Pepsi over rival Coca-Cola.

   a. 1990 Clean Air Act
   b. 28-hour day
   c. 33 Strategies of War
   d. Comparative advertising

Chapter 3. The Internal Environment: Resources, Capabilities, and Core Competencies

4. _____ is something that a firm can do well and that meets the following three conditions:

Competencies are things that companys execute well across several business units or product sectors.

Firms usually have few competencies, but these are usually less liable to change rapidly.

1. It provides consumer benefits
2. It is not easy for competitors to imitate
3. It can be leveraged widely to many products and markets.

A _____ can take various forms, including technical/subject matter know-how, a reliable process and/or close relationships with customers and suppliers (Mascarenhas et al. 1998.)

   a. Learning-by-doing
   b. NAIRU
   c. Dominant Design
   d. Core competency

5. A chief executive officer (_____) or chief executive is one of the highest-ranking corporate officer (executive) or administrator in charge of total management. An individual selected as President and _____ of a corporation, company, organization, or agency, reports to the board of directors. In internal communication and press releases, many companies capitalize the term and those of other high positions, even when they are not proper nouns.
   a. Chief executive officer
   b. Portfolio manager
   c. Director of communications
   d. CEO

6. _____ can be regarded as an outcome of mental processes (cognitive process) leading to the selection of a course of action among several alternatives. Every _____ process produces a final choice. The output can be an action or an opinion of choice.
   a. 33 Strategies of War
   b. 28-hour day
   c. 1990 Clean Air Act
   d. Decision making

7. _____ is a structured approach to transitioning individuals, teams, and organizations from a current state to a desired future state. The current definition of _____ includes both organizational _____ processes and individual _____ models, which together are used to manage the people side of change.

Chapter 3. The Internal Environment: Resources, Capabilities, and Core Competencies

A number of models are available for understanding the transitioning of individuals through the phases of _____ and strengthening organizational development initiative in both government and corporate sectors.

a. 1990 Clean Air Act
b. Change management
c. 33 Strategies of War
d. 28-hour day

8. _____, commonly known as e-commerce, consists of the buying and selling of products or services over electronic systems such as the Internet and other computer networks. The amount of trade conducted electronically has grown extraordinarily with widespread Internet usage. The use of commerce is conducted in this way, spurring and drawing on innovations in electronic funds transfer, supply chain management, Internet marketing, online transaction processing, electronic data interchange (EDI), inventory management systems, and automated data collection systems.

a. A Stake in the Outcome
b. Online shopping
c. A4e
d. Electronic Commerce

9. _____ is an increasingly broadening term with which an organization, or other human system describes the combination of traditionally administrative personnel functions with acquisition and application of skills, knowledge and experience, Employee Relations and resource planning at various levels. The field draws upon concepts developed in Industrial/Organizational Psychology and System Theory. _____ has at least two related interpretations depending on context. The original usage derives from political economy and economics, where it was traditionally called labor, one of four factors of production although this perspective is changing as a function of new and ongoing research into more strategic approaches at national levels. This first usage is used more in terms of '_____ development', and can go beyond just organizations to the level of nations. The more traditional usage within corporations and businesses refers to the individuals within a firm or agency, and to the portion of the organization that deals with hiring, firing, training, and other personnel issues, typically referred to as `_____ management'.

a. Human resource management
b. Bradford Factor
c. Progressive discipline
d. Human resources

10. A _____ is a name or trademark connected with a product or producer. _____s have become increasingly important components of culture and the economy, now being described as 'cultural accessories and personal philosophies'.

Some people distinguish the psychological aspect of a _____ from the experiential aspect.

a. Brand loyalty
b. Brand awareness
c. Brand extension
d. Brand

11. Descriptive _____ assist in describing the distinguishable selling point(s) of the product to the customer (eg Snap Crackle ' Pop or Bitter Lemon.)

Associative _____ provide the customer with an associated word for what the product promises to do or be (e.g. Walkman, Sensodyne or Natrel)

Finally, Freestanding _____ have no links or ties to either descriptions or associations of use. (eg Mars Bar or Pantene)

The act of associating a product or service with a brand has become part of pop culture.

a. Brand image
b. Brand awareness
c. Brand names
d. Brand extension

12. A _____ is the highest-ranking corporate officer concerning talent or learning management of a corporation or agency. _____s can be experts in corporate or personal training, with degrees in education, instructional design or similar.

Qualified _____s of corporations should have leadership skills and be able clearly handle the training management of their company.

a. Chief learning officer
b. Cadbury Report
c. King I
d. Corporate headquarters

13. _____ refers to the stock of skills and knowledge embodied in the ability to perform labor so as to produce economic value. It is the skills and knowledge gained by a worker through education and experience. Many early economic theories refer to it simply as labor, one of three factors of production, and consider it to be a fungible resource -- homogeneous and easily interchangeable.

Chapter 3. The Internal Environment: Resources, Capabilities, and Core Competencies   31

a. Deflation
b. Productivity management
c. Market structure
d. Human capital

14. In business and accounting, _____s are everything of value that is owned by a person or company. Any property or object of value that one possesses, usually considered as applicable to the payment of one's debts is considered an _____. Simplistically stated, _____s are things of value that can be readily converted into cash.

a. A Stake in the Outcome
b. A4e
c. AAAI
d. Asset

15. _____ is an idea in the field of Organizational studies and management which describes the psychology, attitudes, experiences, beliefs and Values (personal and cultural values) of an organization. It has been defined as 'the specific collection of values and norms that are shared by people and groups in an organization and that control the way they interact with each other and with stakeholders outside the organization.'

This definition continues to explain organizational values also known as 'beliefs and ideas about what kinds of goals members of an organization should pursue and ideas about the appropriate kinds or standards of behavior organizational members should use to achieve these goals. From organizational values develop organizational norms, guidelines or expectations that prescribe appropriate kinds of behavior by employees in particular situations and control the behavior of organizational members towards one another.'

_____ is not the same as corporate culture.

a. Organizational development
b. Organizational culture
c. Organizational effectiveness
d. Union shop

16. The loyalty business model is a business model used in strategic management in which company resources are employed so as to increase the loyalty of customers and other stakeholders in the expectation that corporate objectives will be met or surpassed. A typical example of this type of model is: quality of product or service leads to customer satisfaction, which leads to _____, which leads to profitability.

Fredrick Reichheld (1996) expanded the loyalty business model beyond customers and employees.

Chapter 3. The Internal Environment: Resources, Capabilities, and Core Competencies

   a. 33 Strategies of War
   b. 1990 Clean Air Act
   c. 28-hour day
   d. Customer loyalty

17. In marketing, _____ is the process of distinguishing the differences of a product or offering from others, to make it more attractive to a particular target market. This involves differentiating it from competitors' products as well as one's own product offerings.
   a. Market development
   b. Product differentiation
   c. Market share
   d. PEST analysis

18. A _____ is something for which there is demand, but which is supplied without qualitative differentiation across a market. It is a product that is the same no matter who produces it, such as petroleum, notebook paper, or milk. In other words, copper is copper.
   a. 33 Strategies of War
   b. 28-hour day
   c. Commodity
   d. 1990 Clean Air Act

19. _____ according to Onuoha (2007) is the practice of starting new organizations or revitalizing mature organizations, particularly new businesses generally in response to identified opportunities. _____ is often a difficult undertaking, as a vast majority of new businesses fail. Entrepreneurial activities are substantially different depending on the type of organization that is being started.
   a. AAAI
   b. A4e
   c. A Stake in the Outcome
   d. Entrepreneurship

20. In game theory, an _____ is a set of moves or strategies taken by the players, or their payoffs resulting from the actions or strategies taken by all players. The two are complementary in that given knowledge of the set of strategies of all players, the final state of the game is known, as are any relevant payoffs. In a game where chance or a random event is involved, the _____ is not known from only the set of strategies, but is only realized when the random event(s) are realized.

Chapter 3. The Internal Environment: Resources, Capabilities, and Core Competencies

a. A4e
b. A Stake in the Outcome
c. AAAI
d. Outcome

21. The _____ is a concept from business management that was first described and popularized by Michael Porter in his 1985 best-seller, Competitive Advantage: Creating and Sustaining Superior Performance.

A _____ is a chain of activities. Products pass through all activities of the chain in order and at each activity the product gains some value. The chain of activities gives the products more added value than the sum of added values of all activities. It is important not to mix the concept of the _____ with the costs occurring throughout the activities.

a. Market development
b. Mass marketing
c. Customer relationship management
d. Value chain

22. _____ is the management of the flow of goods, information and other resources, including energy and people, between the point of origin and the point of consumption in order to meet the requirements of consumers (frequently, and originally, military organizations.) _____ involves the integration of information, transportation, inventory, warehousing, material-handling, and packaging, and occasionally security. _____ is a channel of the supply chain which adds the value of time and place utility.

a. 28-hour day
b. 1990 Clean Air Act
c. Third-party logistics
d. Logistics

23. _____ is an integrated communications-based process through which individuals and communities discover that existing and newly-identified needs and wants may be satisfied by the products and services of others.

_____ is defined by the American _____ Association as the activity, set of institutions, and processes for creating, communicating, delivering, and exchanging offerings that have value for customers, clients, partners, and society at large. The term developed from the original meaning which referred literally to going to market, as in shopping, or going to a market to buy or sell goods or services.

Chapter 3. The Internal Environment: Resources, Capabilities, and Core Competencies

a. Customer relationship management
b. Market development
c. Marketing
d. Disruptive technology

24. A _____ is a process in which a potential employee is evaluated by an employer for prospective employment in their company, organization and was established in the late 16th century.

A _____ typically precedes the hiring decision, and is used to evaluate the candidate. The interview is usually preceded by the evaluation of submitted résumés from interested candidates, then selecting a small number of candidates for interviews.

a. Job interview
b. Split shift
c. Supported employment
d. Payrolling

25. _____ is subcontracting a process, such as product design or manufacturing, to a third-party company. The decision to outsource is often made in the interest of lowering cost or making better use of time and energy costs, redirecting or conserving energy directed at the competencies of a particular business, or to make more efficient use of land, labor, capital, (information) technology and resources. _____ became part of the business lexicon during the 1980s.

a. Opinion leadership
b. Operant conditioning
c. Unemployment insurance
d. Outsourcing

26. _____ is the acquisition of goods and/or services at the best possible total cost of ownership, in the right quality and quantity, at the right time, in the right place and from the right source for the direct benefit or use of corporations, individuals generally via a contract. Simple _____ may involve nothing more than repeat purchasing. Complex _____ could involve finding long term partners - or even 'co-destiny' suppliers that might fundamentally commit one organization to another.

a. Sole proprietorship
b. Golden parachute
c. Procurement
d. Psychological pricing

27. _____ is the process of research and development of technology. Many emerging technologies are expected to become generally applied in the near future.

The new technology development process leans on the New product development process.

a. 28-hour day
b. 33 Strategies of War
c. 1990 Clean Air Act
d. Technological development

Chapter 4. Business-Level Strategy

1. A _____ is an entity formed between two or more parties to undertake economic activity together. The parties agree to create a new entity by both contributing equity, and they then share in the revenues, expenses, and control of the enterprise. The venture can be for one specific project only, or a continuing business relationship such as the Fuji Xerox _____.
   a. Joint venture
   b. Civil Rights Act of 1991
   c. Meritor Savings Bank v. Vinson
   d. Patent

2. An _____ is a person who has possession of an enterprise and assumes significant accountability for the inherent risks and the outcome. It is an ambitious leader who combines land, labor, and capital to create and market new goods or services. The term is a loanword from French and was first defined by the Irish economist Richard Cantillon.
   a. A Stake in the Outcome
   b. Entrepreneur
   c. A4e
   d. AAAI

3. _____ is a technical term used in management science popularized by Joseph M. Juran

He defined an internal and external customers as anyone affected by the product or by the process used to produce the product, in the context of quality management. _____s may play the role as supplier, processer, and customer in the sequence of product development.

He claimed that the organization must understand and identify both internal and external customers and their needs.

   a. AAAI
   b. A4e
   c. A Stake in the Outcome
   d. Internal customer

4. The loyalty business model is a business model used in strategic management in which company resources are employed so as to increase the loyalty of customers and other stakeholders in the expectation that corporate objectives will be met or surpassed. A typical example of this type of model is: quality of product or service leads to customer satisfaction, which leads to _____, which leads to profitability.

Fredrick Reichheld (1996) expanded the loyalty business model beyond customers and employees.

a. Customer loyalty
b. 28-hour day
c. 33 Strategies of War
d. 1990 Clean Air Act

5. In law, _____ is the term to describe a partnership between two or more parties.

In England a number of statutes on the subject have been passed, the chief being the Bastardy Act of 1845, and the Bastardy Laws Amendment Acts of 1872 and 1873. The mother of a bastard may summon the putative father to petty sessions within twelve months of the birth (or at any later time if he is proved to have contributed to the child's support within twelve months after the birth), and the justices, as after hearing evidence on both sides, may, if the mother's evidence be corroborated in some material particular, adjudge the man to be the putative father of the child, and order him to pay a sum not exceeding five shillings a week for its maintenance, together with a sum for expenses incidental to the birth, or the funeral expenses, if it has died before the date of order, and the costs of the proceedings.

a. Abraham Harold Maslow
b. Affirmative action
c. Affiliation
d. Adam Smith

6. _____ or _____ data refers to selected population characteristics as used in government, marketing or opinion research, or the _____ profiles used in such research. Note the distinction from the term 'demography' Commonly-used _____s include race, age, income, disabilities, mobility (in terms of travel time to work or number of vehicles available), educational attainment, home ownership, employment status, and even location.
a. Affiliation
b. Adam Smith
c. Abraham Harold Maslow
d. Demographic

7. A _____ is a group of people or organizations sharing one or more characteristics that cause them to have similar product and/or service needs. A true _____ meets all of the following criteria: it is distinct from other segments (different segments have different needs), it is homogeneous within the segment (exhibits common needs); it responds similarly to a market stimulus, and it can be reached by a market intervention. The term is also used when consumers with identical product and/or service needs are divided up into groups so they can be charged different amounts.

a. SWOT analysis
b. Customer relationship management
c. Market segment
d. Context analysis

8. _____ is a broad label that refers to any individuals or households that use goods and services generated within the economy. The concept of a _____ is used in different contexts, so that the usage and significance of the term may vary.

Typically when business people and economists talk of _____s they are talking about person as _____, an aggregated commodity item with little individuality other than that expressed in the buy/not-buy decision.

a. 33 Strategies of War
b. 28-hour day
c. 1990 Clean Air Act
d. Consumer

9. _____ for short is a descriptive term for certain executives in a business operation. It is also a formal title held by some business executives, most commonly in the hospitality industry.

A _____ has broad, overall responsibility for a business or organization. Whereas a manager may be responsible for one functional area, the _____ is responsible for all areas.

a. Chief technology officer
b. Chief knowledge officer
c. Managing director
d. General manager

10. _____ is a term used to describe the demographic cohort following Generation X. Its members are often referred to as 'Millennials' or 'Echo Boomers') . There are no precise dates for when Gen Y begins and ends. Most commentators use dates from the early 1980s to early 1990s.
a. Giovanni Agnelli
b. David Wittig
c. Benjamin R. Barber
d. Generation Y

11. _____ is something that a firm can do well and that meets the following three conditions:

Chapter 4. Business-Level Strategy 39

Competencies are things that companys execute well across several business units or product sectors.

Firms usually have few competencies, but these are usually less liable to change rapidly.

1. It provides consumer benefits
2. It is not easy for competitors to imitate
3. It can be leveraged widely to many products and markets.

A _____ can take various forms, including technical/subject matter know-how, a reliable process and/or close relationships with customers and suppliers (Mascarenhas et al. 1998.)

a. NAIRU
b. Learning-by-doing
c. Core competency
d. Dominant Design

12. In marketing, _____ has come to mean the process by which marketers try to create an image or identity in the minds of their target market for its product, brand, or organization. It is the 'relative competitive comparison' their product occupies in a given market as perceived by the target market.

Re-_____ involves changing the identity of a product, relative to the identity of competing products, in the collective minds of the target market.

a. Customer analytics
b. Context analysis
c. PEST analysis
d. Positioning

13. _____ is, in very basic words, a position a firm occupies against its competitors.

According to Michael Porter, the three methods for creating a sustainable _____ are through:

1. Cost leadership

2. Differentiation

3. Focus (economics)

a. 1990 Clean Air Act
b. 28-hour day
c. Theory Z
d. Competitive advantage

14. In economics, business, retail, and accounting, a _____ is the value of money that has been used up to produce something, and hence is not available for use anymore. In economics, a _____ is an alternative that is given up as a result of a decision. In business, the _____ may be one of acquisition, in which case the amount of money expended to acquire it is counted as _____.
   a. Fixed costs
   b. Cost allocation
   c. Cost overrun
   d. Cost

15. _____ is a concept developed by Michael Porter, used in business strategy. It describes a way to establish the competitive advantage. _____, in basic words, means the lowest cost of operation in the industry.
   a. Switching cost
   b. Strategic business unit
   c. Strategic group
   d. Cost leadership

16. _____ has been described as the 'process of social influence in which one person can enlist the aid and support of others in the accomplishment of a common task' . A definition more inclusive of followers comes from Alan Keith of Genentech who said '_____ is ultimately about creating a way for people to contribute to making something extraordinary happen.'

_____ is one of the most salient aspects of the organizational context. However, defining _____ has been challenging.

   a. Leadership
   b. 28-hour day
   c. Situational leadership
   d. 1990 Clean Air Act

Chapter 4. Business-Level Strategy 41

17. _____ is the management of the flow of goods, information and other resources, including energy and people, between the point of origin and the point of consumption in order to meet the requirements of consumers (frequently, and originally, military organizations.) _____ involves the integration of information, transportation, inventory, warehousing, material-handling, and packaging, and occasionally security. _____ is a channel of the supply chain which adds the value of time and place utility.

a. 1990 Clean Air Act
b. Third-party logistics
c. 28-hour day
d. Logistics

18. _____ is a concept related to the relative abilities of parties in a situation to exert influence over each other. If both parties are on an equal footing in a debate, then they will have equal _____, such as in a perfectly competitive market, or between an evenly matched monopoly and monopsony.

There are a number of fields where the concept of _____ has proven crucial to coherent analysis: game theory, labour economics, collective bargaining arrangements, diplomatic negotiations, settlement of litigation, the price of insurance, and any negotiation in general.

a. 1990 Clean Air Act
b. Trade credit
c. Buy-sell agreement
d. Bargaining power

19. In decision theory and estimation theory, the _____ of an estimator, $\hat{\theta}$, of an unknown parameter of the distribution, θ, is the expected value of the loss function

$$R(\theta, \hat{\theta}) = \mathbb{E}_\theta L(\theta, \hat{\theta}) = \int L(\theta, \hat{\theta})\, dP_\theta.$$

where dP_θ is a probability measure parametrized by θ.

- For a scalar parameter θ and a quadratic loss function,

$$L(\theta, \hat{\theta}) = (\theta - \hat{\theta})^2$$

the _____ function becomes the mean squared error of the estimate,

$$R(\theta, \hat{\theta}) = E_\theta (\theta - \hat{\theta})^2$$

- In density estimation, the unknown parameter is probability density itself. The loss function is typically chosen to be a norm in an appropriate function space. For example, for L^2 norm,

$$L(f, \hat{f}) = \|f - \hat{f}\|_2^2$$

the _____ function becomes the mean integrated squared error

$$R(f, \hat{f}) = E\|f - \hat{f}\|^2$$

a. Risk
b. Financial modeling
c. Risk aversion
d. Linear model

20. The _____ is a concept from business management that was first described and popularized by Michael Porter in his 1985 best-seller, Competitive Advantage: Creating and Sustaining Superior Performance.

A _____ is a chain of activities. Products pass through all activities of the chain in order and at each activity the product gains some value. The chain of activities gives the products more added value than the sum of added values of all activities. It is important not to mix the concept of the _____ with the costs occurring throughout the activities.

a. Customer relationship management
b. Market development
c. Mass marketing
d. Value chain

21. A _____ is a name or trademark connected with a product or producer. _____s have become increasingly important components of culture and the economy, now being described as 'cultural accessories and personal philosophies'.

Some people distinguish the psychological aspect of a _____ from the experiential aspect.

　a. Brand extension
　b. Brand
　c. Brand loyalty
　d. Brand awareness

22. _____, in marketing, consists of a consumer's commitment to repurchase or otherwise continue using the brand and can be demonstrated by repeated buying of a product or service or other positive behaviors such as word of mouth advocacy.

_____ is more than simple repurchasing, however. Customers may repurchase a brand due to situational constraints, a lack of viable alternatives, or out of convenience.

　a. Brand awareness
　b. Brand image
　c. Brand loyalty
　d. Brand extension

23. _____ Management is the succession of strategies used by management as a product goes through its _____. The conditions in which a product is sold changes over time and must be managed as it moves through its succession of stages.

The _____ goes through many phases, involves many professional disciplines, and requires many skills, tools and processes.

　a. Job hunting
　b. Golden handshake
　c. Product life cycle
　d. Strategic Alliance

24. A _____ system is a manufacturing system in which there is some amount of flexibility that allows the system to react in the case of changes, whether predicted or unpredicted. This flexibility is generally considered to fall into two categories, which both contain numerous subcategories.

The first category, machine flexibility, covers the system's ability to be changed to produce new product types, and ability to change the order of operations executed on a part. The second category is called routing flexibility, which consists of the ability to use multiple machines to perform the same operation on a part, as well as the system's ability to absorb large-scale changes, such as in volume, capacity, or capability.

a. Jidoka
b. Homeworkers
c. Manufacturing resource planning
d. Flexible manufacturing

25. _____ consists of the processes a company uses to track and organize its contacts with its current and prospective customers. _____ software is used to support these processes; information about customers and customer interactions can be entered, stored and accessed by employees in different company departments. Typical _____ goals are to improve services provided to customers, and to use customer contact information for targeted marketing.

a. Marketing plan
b. Green marketing
c. Disruptive technology
d. Customer relationship management

26. _____ can be considered to have three main components: quality control, quality assurance and quality improvement. _____ is focused not only on product quality, but also the means to achieve it. _____ therefore uses quality assurance and control of processes as well as products to achieve more consistent quality.

a. Total quality management
b. Quality management
c. 28-hour day
d. 1990 Clean Air Act

27. _____ is a business management strategy aimed at embedding awareness of quality in all organizational processes. _____ has been widely used in manufacturing, education, hospitals, call centers, government, and service industries, as well as NASA space and science programs.

As defined by the International Organization for Standardization (ISO):

> '_____ is a management approach for an organization, centered on quality, based on the participation of all its members and aiming at long-term success through customer satisfaction, and benefits to all members of the organization and to society.' ISO 8402:1994

One major aim is to reduce variation from every process so that greater consistency of effort is obtained. (Royse, D., Thyer, B., Padgett D., ' Logan T., 2006)

a. 1990 Clean Air Act
b. 28-hour day
c. Quality management
d. Total quality management

28. A _____ is a commercial building for storage of goods. _____s are used by manufacturers, importers, exporters, wholesalers, transport businesses, customs, etc. They are usually large plain buildings in industrial areas of cities and towns.
a. 33 Strategies of War
b. 28-hour day
c. 1990 Clean Air Act
d. Warehouse

Chapter 5. Competitive Rivalry and Competitive Dynamics

1. An _____ is a person who has possession of an enterprise and assumes significant accountability for the inherent risks and the outcome. It is an ambitious leader who combines land, labor, and capital to create and market new goods or services. The term is a loanword from French and was first defined by the Irish economist Richard Cantillon.
    a. AAAI
    b. Entrepreneur
    c. A Stake in the Outcome
    d. A4e

2. In economics and especially in the theory of competition, _____ are obstacles in the path of a firm that make it difficult to enter a given market.

    _____ are the source of a firm's pricing power - the ability of a firm to raise prices without losing all its customers.

    The term refers to hindrances that an individual may face while trying to gain entrance into a profession or trade.

    a. 1990 Clean Air Act
    b. 28-hour day
    c. Predatory pricing
    d. Barriers to entry

3. _____ in marketing and strategic management is an assessment of the strengths and weaknesses of current and potential competitors. This analysis provides both an offensive and defensive strategic context through which to identify opportunities and threats. Competitor profiling coalesces all of the relevant sources of _____ into one framework in the support of efficient and effective strategy formulation, implementation, monitoring and adjustment.
    a. Competitor or Competitive Intelligence
    b. 1990 Clean Air Act
    c. 28-hour day
    d. Competitor analysis

4. _____ is an advertisement in which a particular product specifically mentions a competitor by name for the express purpose of showing why the competitor is inferior to the product naming it.

    This should not be confused with parody advertisements, where a fictional product is being advertised for the purpose of poking fun at the particular advertisement, nor should it be confused with the use of a coined brand name for the purpose of comparing the product without actually naming an actual competitor. ('Wikipedia tastes better and is less filling than the Encyclopedia Galactica.')

    In the 1980s, during what has been referred to as the cola wars, soft-drink manufacturer Pepsi ran a series of advertisements where people, caught on hidden camera, in a blind taste test, chose Pepsi over rival Coca-Cola.

a. 33 Strategies of War
b. 28-hour day
c. Comparative advertising
d. 1990 Clean Air Act

5. _____ is the advantage gained by the initial occupant of a market segment. This advantage may stem from the fact that the first entrant can gain control of resources that followers may not be able to match. Sometimes the first mover is not able to capitalise on its advantage, leaving the opportunity for another firm to gain second-mover advantage.
   a. Customer retention
   b. Business ecosystem
   c. Horizontal integration
   d. First-mover advantage

6. In economics and sociology, an _____ is any factor (financial or non-financial) that enables or motivates a particular course of action, or counts as a reason for preferring one choice to the alternatives. It is an expectation that encourages people to behave in a certain way. Since human beings are purposeful creatures, the study of _____ structures is central to the study of all economic activity (both in terms of individual decision-making and in terms of co-operation and competition within a larger institutional structure.)
   a. A4e
   b. AAAI
   c. A Stake in the Outcome
   d. Incentive

7. _____ is a broad label that refers to any individuals or households that use goods and services generated within the economy. The concept of a _____ is used in different contexts, so that the usage and significance of the term may vary.

Typically when business people and economists talk of _____s they are talking about person as _____, an aggregated commodity item with little individuality other than that expressed in the buy/not-buy decision.

   a. 1990 Clean Air Act
   b. Consumer
   c. 33 Strategies of War
   d. 28-hour day

8. The _____ is an agency of the United States Department of Health and Human Services and is responsible for regulating and supervising the safety of foods, dietary supplements, drugs, vaccines, biological medical products, blood products, medical devices, radiation-emitting devices, veterinary products, and cosmetics. The FDA also enforces section 361 of the Public Health Service Act and the associated regulations, including sanitation requirements on interstate travel as well as specific rules for control of disease on products ranging from pet turtles to semen donations for assisted reproductive medicine techniques.

The FDA is an agency within the United States Department of Health and Human Services responsible for protecting and promoting the nation's public health.

a. 28-hour day
b. 33 Strategies of War
c. 1990 Clean Air Act
d. Food and Drug Administration

9. A _____ is a set of exclusive rights granted by a state to an inventor or his assignee for a limited period of time in exchange for a disclosure of an invention.

The procedure for granting _____s, the requirements placed on the _____ee and the extent of the exclusive rights vary widely between countries according to national laws and international agreements. Typically, however, a _____ application must include one or more claims defining the invention which must be new, inventive, and useful or industrially applicable.

a. Food, Drug, and Cosmetic Act
b. Patent
c. Federal Trade Commission Act
d. Labor Management Reporting and Disclosure Act

10. _____ is the process of discovering the technological principles of a device, object or system through analysis of its structure, function and operation. It often involves taking something (e.g., a mechanical device, electronic component, or software program) apart and analyzing its workings in detail to be used in maintenance, or to try to make a new device or program that does the same thing without copying anything from the original.

_____ has its origins in the analysis of hardware for commercial or military advantage .

a. Predictive maintenance
b. 28-hour day
c. 1990 Clean Air Act
d. Reverse engineering

Chapter 5. Competitive Rivalry and Competitive Dynamics

11. The phrase mergers and _____s refers to the aspect of corporate strategy, corporate finance and management dealing with the buying, selling and combining of different companies that can aid, finance, or help a growing company in a given industry grow rapidly without having to create another business entity.

An _____, also known as a takeover or a buyout, is the buying of one company (the 'target') by another. An _____ may be friendly or hostile.

a. A Stake in the Outcome
b. AAAI
c. A4e
d. Acquisition

12. _____ is the process by which a new idea or new product is accepted by the market. The rate of _____ is the speed that the new idea spreads from one consumer to the next. Adoption is similar to _____ except that it deals with the psychological processes an individual goes through, rather than an aggregate market process.
a. Mass marketing
b. Category management
c. Value chain
d. Diffusion

13. _____ is, in very basic words, a position a firm occupies against its competitors.

According to Michael Porter, the three methods for creating a sustainable _____ are through:

1. Cost leadership

2. Differentiation

3. Focus (economics)

a. 1990 Clean Air Act
b. Theory Z
c. 28-hour day
d. Competitive advantage

Chapter 6. Corporate-Level Strategy

1. _____ refers to the aggregated strategies of single business firm or a strategic business unit (SBU) in a diversified corporation. According to Michael Porter, a firm must formulate a _____ that incorporates either cost leadership, differentiation or focus in order to achieve a sustainable competitive advantage and long-term success in its chosen arenas or industries.

Functional strategies include marketing strategies, new product development strategies, human resource strategies, financial strategies, legal strategies, supply-chain strategies, and information technology management strategies.

   a. Competitive heterogeneity
   b. Strategic thinking
   c. Switching cost
   d. Business strategy

2. _____ are conceptually similar to economies of scale. Whereas economies of scale primarily refer to efficiencies associated with supply-side changes, such as increasing or decreasing the scale of production, of a single product type, _____ refer to efficiencies primarily associated with demand-side changes, such as increasing or decreasing the scope of marketing and distribution, of different types of products. _____ are one of the main reasons for such marketing strategies as product bundling, product lining, and family branding.
   a. Economies of scope
   b. A4e
   c. A Stake in the Outcome
   d. Economies of scale

3. In economics and sociology, an _____ is any factor (financial or non-financial) that enables or motivates a particular course of action, or counts as a reason for preferring one choice to the alternatives. It is an expectation that encourages people to behave in a certain way. Since human beings are purposeful creatures, the study of _____ structures is central to the study of all economic activity (both in terms of individual decision-making and in terms of co-operation and competition within a larger institutional structure.)
   a. A Stake in the Outcome
   b. AAAI
   c. A4e
   d. Incentive

4. The phrase mergers and _____s refers to the aspect of corporate strategy, corporate finance and management dealing with the buying, selling and combining of different companies that can aid, finance, or help a growing company in a given industry grow rapidly without having to create another business entity.

An _____, also known as a takeover or a buyout, is the buying of one company (the 'target') by another. An _____ may be friendly or hostile.

Chapter 6. Corporate-Level Strategy

a. A4e
b. AAAI
c. A Stake in the Outcome
d. Acquisition

5. _____ is something that a firm can do well and that meets the following three conditions:

Competencies are things that companys execute well across several business units or product sectors.

Firms usually have few competencies, but these are usually less liable to change rapidly.

1. It provides consumer benefits
2. It is not easy for competitors to imitate
3. It can be leveraged widely to many products and markets.

A _____ can take various forms, including technical/subject matter know-how, a reliable process and/or close relationships with customers and suppliers (Mascarenhas et al. 1998.)

a. Dominant Design
b. Learning-by-doing
c. NAIRU
d. Core competency

6. _____ is used in marketing to describe the inability to assess the value gained from engaging in an activity using any tangible evidence. It is often used to describe services where there isn't a tangible product that the customer can purchase, that can be seen, tasted or touched.

Other key characteristics of services include perishability, inseparability and variability.

a. Up-selling
b. A Stake in the Outcome
c. A4e
d. Intangibility

7. _____ refers to the methods of practicing and using another person's business philosophy. The franchisor grants the independent operator the right to distribute its products, techniques, and trademarks for a percentage of gross monthly sales and a royalty fee. Various tangibles and intangibles such as national or international advertising, training, and other support services are commonly made available by the franchisor.

a. 1990 Clean Air Act
b. 28-hour day
c. Franchising
d. ServiceMaster

8. A _____ is an entity formed between two or more parties to undertake economic activity together. The parties agree to create a new entity by both contributing equity, and they then share in the revenues, expenses, and control of the enterprise. The venture can be for one specific project only, or a continuing business relationship such as the Fuji Xerox _____.
   a. Civil Rights Act of 1991
   b. Patent
   c. Meritor Savings Bank v. Vinson
   d. Joint venture

9. _____ is an advertisement in which a particular product specifically mentions a competitor by name for the express purpose of showing why the competitor is inferior to the product naming it.

This should not be confused with parody advertisements, where a fictional product is being advertised for the purpose of poking fun at the particular advertisement, nor should it be confused with the use of a coined brand name for the purpose of comparing the product without actually naming an actual competitor. ('Wikipedia tastes better and is less filling than the Encyclopedia Galactica.')

In the 1980s, during what has been referred to as the cola wars, soft-drink manufacturer Pepsi ran a series of advertisements where people, caught on hidden camera, in a blind taste test, chose Pepsi over rival Coca-Cola.

   a. 33 Strategies of War
   b. 1990 Clean Air Act
   c. 28-hour day
   d. Comparative advertising

10. An _____ is a person who has possession of an enterprise and assumes significant accountability for the inherent risks and the outcome. It is an ambitious leader who combines land, labor, and capital to create and market new goods or services. The term is a loanword from French and was first defined by the Irish economist Richard Cantillon.
   a. A4e
   b. A Stake in the Outcome
   c. AAAI
   d. Entrepreneur

Chapter 6. Corporate-Level Strategy

11. _____ , also referred to simply as a 'public offering' or 'flotation,' is when a company issues common stock or shares to the public for the first time. They are often issued by smaller, younger companies seeking capital to expand, but can also be done by large privately-owned companies looking to become publicly traded.

In an _____ the issuer may obtain the assistance of an underwriting firm, which helps it determine what type of security to issue (common or preferred), best offering price and time to bring it to market.

a. Occupational Safety and Health Administration
b. Unemployment insurance
c. Outsourcing
d. Initial public offering

12. The _____ or gross domestic income (GDI), a basic measure of an economy's economic performance, is the market value of all final goods and services made within the borders of a nation in a year. _____ can be defined in three ways, all of which are conceptually identical. First, it is equal to the total expenditures for all final goods and services produced within the country in a stipulated period of time (usually a 365-day year).

a. Human capital
b. Perfect competition
c. Gross domestic product
d. Productivity management

13. In microeconomics and management, the term _____ describes a style of management control. Vertically integrated companies are united through a hierarchy with a common owner. Usually each member of the hierarchy produces a different product or (market-specific) service, and the products combine to satisfy a common need.

a. Vertical integration
b. 1990 Clean Air Act
c. 33 Strategies of War
d. 28-hour day

14. _____ is, in very basic words, a position a firm occupies against its competitors.

According to Michael Porter, the three methods for creating a sustainable _____ are through:

1. Cost leadership

2. Differentiation

3. Focus (economics)

Chapter 6. Corporate-Level Strategy

   a. 28-hour day
   b. 1990 Clean Air Act
   c. Competitive advantage
   d. Theory Z

15. _____, commonly known as e-commerce, consists of the buying and selling of products or services over electronic systems such as the Internet and other computer networks. The amount of trade conducted electronically has grown extraordinarily with widespread Internet usage. The use of commerce is conducted in this way, spurring and drawing on innovations in electronic funds transfer, supply chain management, Internet marketing, online transaction processing, electronic data interchange (EDI), inventory management systems, and automated data collection systems.
   a. A4e
   b. Electronic Commerce
   c. Online shopping
   d. A Stake in the Outcome

16. _____ is a concept related to the relative abilities of parties in a situation to exert influence over each other. If both parties are on an equal footing in a debate, then they will have equal _____, such as in a perfectly competitive market, or between an evenly matched monopoly and monopsony.

There are a number of fields where the concept of _____ has proven crucial to coherent analysis: game theory, labour economics, collective bargaining arrangements, diplomatic negotiations, settlement of litigation, the price of insurance, and any negotiation in general.

   a. Trade credit
   b. 1990 Clean Air Act
   c. Buy-sell agreement
   d. Bargaining power

17. _____ is the process of dispersing decision-making governance closer to the people or citizen. It includes the dispersal of administration or governance in sectors or areas like engineering, management science, political science, political economy, sociology and economics. _____ is also possible in the dispersal of population and employment.
   a. Business plan
   b. Frenemy
   c. Formula for Change
   d. Decentralization

Chapter 6. Corporate-Level Strategy

18. A _____ is a security issued by a parent company to track the results of one of its subsidiaries or lines of business. The financial results of the subsidiary or line of business are attributed to the _____. Often, the reason for doing so is to separate a high-growth division from a larger parent company.
   a. 1990 Clean Air Act
   b. 28-hour day
   c. 33 Strategies of War
   d. Tracking stock

19. _____ is the corporate management term for the act of reorganizing the legal, ownership, operational, or other structures of a company for the purpose of making it more profitable, or better organized for its present needs. Alternate reasons for _____ include a change of ownership or ownership structure, demerger repositioning debt _____ and financial _____.
   a. Market value
   b. Net worth
   c. Market value added
   d. Restructuring

20. _____ systems are rule-based systems that are able to automatically provide solutions to repetitive management problems (Turban, Leidner, McLean and Wetherbe, 2007.) _____s are very closely related to business informatics and business analytics.

   _____ systems are based on business rules.

   a. Efficient Consumer Response
   b. Entertainment Management
   c. Executive development
   d. Automated decision support

21. _____ refers to the movement of cash into or out of a business or financial product. It is usually measured during a specified, finite period of time. Measurement of _____ can be used

   - to determine a project's rate of return or value. The time of _____s into and out of projects are used as inputs in financial models such as internal rate of return, and net present value.
   - to determine problems with a business's liquidity. Being profitable does not necessarily mean being liquid. A company can fail because of a shortage of cash, even while profitable.
   - as an alternate measure of a business's profits when it is believed that accrual accounting concepts do not represent economic realities. For example, a company may be notionally profitable but generating little operational cash (as may be the case for a company that barters its products rather than selling for cash.) In such a case, the company may be deriving additional operating cash by issuing shares evaluating default risk, re-investment requirements, etc.

_____ is a generic term used differently depending on the context. It may be defined by users for their own purposes.

a. Sweat equity
b. Gross profit margin
c. Gross profit
d. Cash flow

22. _____ is a term used in accounting, economics and finance to spread the cost of an asset over the span of several years.

In simple words we can say that _____ is the reduction in the value of an asset due to usage, passage of time, wear and tear, technological outdating or obsolescence, depletion, inadequacy, rot, rust, decay or other such factors.

In accounting, _____ is a term used to describe any method of attributing the historical or purchase cost of an asset across its useful life, roughly corresponding to normal wear and tear.

a. Net profit
b. Treasury stock
c. Matching principle
d. Depreciation

23. _____s are payments made by a corporation to its shareholders. It is the portion of corporate profits paid out to stockholders. When a corporation earns a profit or surplus, that money can be put to two uses: it can either be re-invested in the business (called retained earnings), or it can be paid to the shareholders as a _____.

a. 1990 Clean Air Act
b. 33 Strategies of War
c. 28-hour day
d. Dividend

24. The _____ is a private, not-for-profit organization whose primary purpose is to develop generally accepted accounting principles (GAAP) within the United States in the public's interest. The Securities and Exchange Commission (SEC) designated the _____ as the organization responsible for setting accounting standards for public companies in the U.S. It was created in 1973, replacing the Committee on Accounting Procedure (CAP) and the Accounting Principles Board (APB) of the American Institute of Certified Public Accountants (AICPA.)

Chapter 6. Corporate-Level Strategy 57

The _____'s mission is 'to establish and improve standards of financial accounting and reporting for the guidance and education of the public, including issuers, auditors, and users of financial information.' To achieve this, _____ has five goals:

- Improve the usefulness of financial reporting by focusing on the primary characteristics of relevance and reliability, and on the qualities of comparability and consistency.
- Keep standards current to reflect changes in methods of doing business and in the economy.
- Consider promptly any significant areas of deficiency in financial reporting that might be improved through standard setting.
- Promote international convergence of accounting standards concurrent with improving the quality of financial reporting.
- Improve common understanding of the nature and purposes of information in financial reports.

The _____ is not a governmental body. The SEC has legal authority to establish financial accounting and reporting standards for publicly held companies under the Securities Exchange Act of 1934.

a. Financial Accounting Standards Board
b. Foreign direct investment
c. Prospero Business Suite
d. Chief risk officer

25. In corporate finance, _____ is cash flow available for distribution among all the securities holders of an organization. They include equity holders, debt holders, preferred stock holders, convertible security holders, and so on.

Note that the first three lines above are calculated for you on the standard Statement of Cash Flows.

a. Kaizen
b. Policies and procedures
c. Free cash flow
d. Pre-determined overhead rate

26. In economics, a _____ is the combination of two or more firms competing in the same market with the same good or service. See Horizontal integration.
a. 28-hour day
b. 1990 Clean Air Act
c. 33 Strategies of War
d. Horizontal merger

Chapter 6. Corporate-Level Strategy

27. _____ in the UK (meaning acquisitions of public companies only) are governed by the City Code on _____ and Mergers, also known as the 'City Code' or 'Takeover Code'. The rules for a takeover, can be found what is primarily known as 'The Blue Book'. The Code used to be a non-statutory set of rules that was controlled by City institutions on a theoretically voluntary basis.
   a. 28-hour day
   b. 33 Strategies of War
   c. 1990 Clean Air Act
   d. Takeovers

28. The _____ of an edge is $c_f(u, v) = c(u, v) - f(u, v)$. This defines a residual network denoted $G_f(V, E_f)$, giving the amount of available capacity. See that there can be an edge from u to v in the residual network, even though there is no edge from u to v in the original network.
   a. 1990 Clean Air Act
   b. Residual capacity
   c. 28-hour day
   d. 33 Strategies of War

29. _____ is the removal or simplification of government rules and regulations that constrain the operation of market forces. _____ does not mean elimination of laws against fraud, but eliminating or reducing government control of how business is done, thereby moving toward a more free market.

The stated rationale for '_____' is often that fewer and simpler regulations will lead to a raised level of competitiveness, therefore higher productivity, more efficiency and lower prices overall.

   a. Value added
   b. Natural rate of unemployment
   c. Rehn-Meidner Model
   d. Deregulation

30. In finance and economics, _____ or divestiture is the reduction of some kind of asset for either financial or ethical objectives or sale of an existing business by a firm. A _____ is the opposite of an investment.
   a. 28-hour day
   b. 33 Strategies of War
   c. Divestment
   d. 1990 Clean Air Act

31. _____ is the state or fact of exclusive rights and control over property, which may be an object, land/real estate or intellectual property. An _____ right is also referred to as title. The concept of _____ has existed for thousands of years and in all cultures.
   a. Emanation of the state
   b. A Stake in the Outcome
   c. A4e
   d. Ownership

32. A _____ is a process in which a potential employee is evaluated by an employer for prospective employment in their company, organization and was established in the late 16th century.

A _____ typically precedes the hiring decision, and is used to evaluate the candidate. The interview is usually preceded by the evaluation of submitted résumés from interested candidates, then selecting a small number of candidates for interviews.

   a. Job interview
   b. Split shift
   c. Supported employment
   d. Payrolling

33. In decision theory and estimation theory, the _____ of an estimator, $\hat{\theta}$, of an unknown parameter of the distribution, θ, is the expected value of the loss function

$$R(\theta, \hat{\theta}) = \mathbb{E}_\theta L(\theta, \hat{\theta}) = \int L(\theta, \hat{\theta})\, dP_\theta.$$

where dP_θ is a probability measure parametrized by θ.

- For a scalar parameter θ and a quadratic loss function,

$$L(\theta, \hat{\theta}) = (\theta - \hat{\theta})^2$$

the _____ function becomes the mean squared error of the estimate,

$$R(\theta, \hat{\theta}) = E_\theta (\theta - \hat{\theta})^2$$

- In density estimation, the unknown parameter is probability density itself. The loss function is typically chosen to be a norm in an appropriate function space. For example, for L^2 norm,

$$L(f, \hat{f}) = \|f - \hat{f}\|_2^2$$

the _____ function becomes the mean integrated squared error

$$R(f, \hat{f}) = E\|f - \hat{f}\|^2$$

a. Financial modeling
b. Risk aversion
c. Risk
d. Linear model

34. _____ is the term used to describe a situation where different entities cooperate advantageously for a final outcome. Simply defined, it means that the whole is greater than the sum of the individual parts. Although the whole will be greater than each individual part, this is not the concept of _____.
   a. 1990 Clean Air Act
   b. 28-hour day
   c. 33 Strategies of War
   d. Synergy

35. A chief executive officer (_____) or chief executive is one of the highest-ranking corporate officer (executive) or administrator in charge of total management. An individual selected as President and _____ of a corporation, company, organization, or agency, reports to the board of directors. In internal communication and press releases, many companies capitalize the term and those of other high positions, even when they are not proper nouns.

a. Director of communications
b. Portfolio manager
c. CEO
d. Chief executive officer

36. _____ is a contract between two parties, one being the employer and the other being the employee. An employee may be defined as: 'A person in the service of another under any contract of hire, express or implied, oral or written, where the employer has the power or right to control and direct the employee in the material details of how the work is to be performed.' Black's Law Dictionary page 471 (5th ed. 1979.)
    a. Employment rate
    b. Employment
    c. Employment counsellor
    d. Exit interview

37. _____ is how top executives of business corporations are paid. This includes a basic salary, bonuses, shares, options and other company benefits. Over the past three decades, _____ has risen dramatically beyond the rising levels of an average worker's wage.
    a. Association management company
    b. Anti-leadership
    c. Evidence-based management
    d. Executive compensation

38. A _____ is an agreement between a company and an employee (usually upper executive) specifying that the employee will receive certain significant benefits if employment is terminated. Sometimes, certain conditions, typically a change in company ownership, must be met, but often the cause of termination is unspecified. These benefits may include severance pay, cash bonuses, stock options, or other benefits.
    a. Career development
    b. Job hunting
    c. First-mover advantage
    d. Golden parachute

39. _____ is a term referring to any strategy, generally in business or politics, to increase the likelihood of negative results over positive ones for a party that attempts any kind of takeover. It derives from its original meaning of a literal _____ carried by various spies throughout history, taken when discovered to eliminate the possibility of being interrogated for the enemy's gain.

In publicly held companies, various methods to avoid takeover bids are called '_____s'.

a. 28-hour day
b. 1990 Clean Air Act
c. 33 Strategies of War
d. Poison pill

Chapter 7. Acquisition and Restructuring Strategies

1. The phrase mergers and _____s refers to the aspect of corporate strategy, corporate finance and management dealing with the buying, selling and combining of different companies that can aid, finance, or help a growing company in a given industry grow rapidly without having to create another business entity.

An _____, also known as a takeover or a buyout, is the buying of one company (the 'target') by another. An _____ may be friendly or hostile.

   a. Acquisition
   b. A4e
   c. AAAI
   d. A Stake in the Outcome

2. _____ in the UK (meaning acquisitions of public companies only) are governed by the City Code on _____ and Mergers, also known as the 'City Code' or 'Takeover Code'. The rules for a takeover, can be found what is primarily known as 'The Blue Book'. The Code used to be a non-statutory set of rules that was controlled by City institutions on a theoretically voluntary basis.
   a. 33 Strategies of War
   b. 28-hour day
   c. 1990 Clean Air Act
   d. Takeovers

3. _____ is a term referring to any strategy, generally in business or politics, to increase the likelihood of negative results over positive ones for a party that attempts any kind of takeover. It derives from its original meaning of a literal _____ carried by various spies throughout history, taken when discovered to eliminate the possibility of being interrogated for the enemy's gain.

In publicly held companies, various methods to avoid takeover bids are called '_____s'.

   a. 1990 Clean Air Act
   b. 28-hour day
   c. 33 Strategies of War
   d. Poison pill

4. _____ is the branch of economics that studies the dynamics of exchange rates, foreign investment, and how these affect international trade. It also studies international projects, international investments and capital flows, and trade deficits. It includes the study of futures, options and currency swaps.

a. A4e
b. AAAI
c. A Stake in the Outcome
d. International finance

5. In business and engineering, new _____ is the term used to describe the complete process of bringing a new product or service to market. There are two parallel paths involved in the NProduct development process: one involves the idea generation, product design, and detail engineering; the other involves market research and marketing analysis. Companies typically see new _____ as the first stage in generating and commercializing new products within the overall strategic process of product life cycle management used to maintain or grow their market share.

a. 28-hour day
b. 1990 Clean Air Act
c. 33 Strategies of War
d. Product development

6. In economics, business, retail, and accounting, a _____ is the value of money that has been used up to produce something, and hence is not available for use anymore. In economics, a _____ is an alternative that is given up as a result of a decision. In business, the _____ may be one of acquisition, in which case the amount of money expended to acquire it is counted as _____.

a. Cost allocation
b. Fixed costs
c. Cost overrun
d. Cost

7. _____ is technology based on biology, especially when used in agriculture, food science, and medicine. United Nations Convention on Biological Diversity defines _____ as:

_____ is often used to refer to genetic engineering technology of the 21st century, however the term encompasses a wider range and history of procedures for modifying biological organisms according to the needs of humanity, going back to the initial modifications of native plants into improved food crops through artificial selection and hybridization. Bioengineering is the science upon which all biotechnological applications are based.

a. 33 Strategies of War
b. 28-hour day
c. Biotechnology
d. 1990 Clean Air Act

Chapter 7. Acquisition and Restructuring Strategies

8. A _____ is a process in which a potential employee is evaluated by an employer for prospective employment in their company, organization and was established in the late 16th century.

A _____ typically precedes the hiring decision, and is used to evaluate the candidate. The interview is usually preceded by the evaluation of submitted résumés from interested candidates, then selecting a small number of candidates for interviews.

a. Job interview
b. Split shift
c. Payrolling
d. Supported employment

9. A _____ strategy is the planned method of delivering goods or services to a target market and distributing them there. When importing or exporting services, it refers to establishing and managing contracts in a foreign country.

Many companies successfully operate in a niche market without ever expanding into new markets.

a. Horizontal integration
b. Psychological pricing
c. Foreign ownership
d. Market entry

10. In decision theory and estimation theory, the _____ of an estimator, $\hat{\theta}$, of an unknown parameter of the distribution, θ, is the expected value of the loss function

$$R(\theta, \hat{\theta}) = \mathbb{E}_\theta L(\theta, \hat{\theta}) = \int L(\theta, \hat{\theta})\, dP_\theta.$$

where dP_θ is a probability measure parametrized by θ.

- For a scalar parameter θ and a quadratic loss function,

$$L(\theta, \hat{\theta}) = (\theta - \hat{\theta})^2$$

the _____ function becomes the mean squared error of the estimate,

$$R(\theta, \hat{\theta}) = E_\theta(\theta - \hat{\theta})^2$$

- In density estimation, the unknown parameter is probability density itself. The loss function is typically chosen to be a norm in an appropriate function space. For example, for L^2 norm,

$$L(f, \hat{f}) = \|f - \hat{f}\|_2^2$$

the _____ function becomes the mean integrated squared error

$$R(f, \hat{f}) = E\|f - \hat{f}\|^2$$

a. Linear model
b. Risk aversion
c. Financial modeling
d. Risk

11. A chief executive officer (_____) or chief executive is one of the highest-ranking corporate officer (executive) or administrator in charge of total management. An individual selected as President and _____ of a corporation, company, organization, or agency, reports to the board of directors. In internal communication and press releases, many companies capitalize the term and those of other high positions, even when they are not proper nouns.
    a. Director of communications
    b. Chief executive officer
    c. Portfolio manager
    d. CEO

12. A _____ is a special kind of database for knowledge management, providing the means for the computerized collection, organization, and retrieval of knowledge.

Chapter 7. Acquisition and Restructuring Strategies 67

_____s are categorized into two major types:

- Machine-readable _____s store knowledge in a computer-readable form, usually for the purpose of having automated deductive reasoning applied to them. They contain a set of data, often in the form of rules that describe the knowledge in a logically consistent manner. An ontology can define the structure of stored data - what types of entities are recorded and what their relationships are. Logical operators, such as And (conjunction), Or (disjunction), material implication and negation may be used to build it up from simpler pieces of information. Consequently, classical deduction can be used to reason about the knowledge in the _____. Some machine-readable _____s are used with artificial intelligence, for example as part of an expert system that focuses on a domain like prescription drugs or customs law. Such _____s are also used by the semantic web.

- Human-readable _____s are designed to allow people to retrieve and use the knowledge they contain. They are commonly used to complement a help desk or for sharing information among employees within an organization. They might store troubleshooting information, articles, white papers, user manuals, or answers to frequently asked questions.

a. Knowledge base
b. 28-hour day
c. 1990 Clean Air Act
d. 33 Strategies of War

13. _____ is a term used for a number of concepts involving either the performance of an investigation of a business or person, or the performance of an act with a certain standard of care. It can be a legal obligation, but the term will more commonly apply to voluntary investigations. A common example of _____ in various industries is the process through which a potential acquirer evaluates a target company or its assets for acquisition.
    a. Flextime
    b. Negligence in employment
    c. Technology transfer
    d. Due diligence

14. _____ refers to the stock of skills and knowledge embodied in the ability to perform labor so as to produce economic value. It is the skills and knowledge gained by a worker through education and experience. Many early economic theories refer to it simply as labor, one of three factors of production, and consider it to be a fungible resource -- homogeneous and easily interchangeable.

a. Human capital
b. Productivity management
c. Deflation
d. Market structure

15. _____ is a legally declared inability or impairment of ability of an individual or organization to pay its creditors. Creditors may file a _____ petition against a debtor ('involuntary _____') in an effort to recoup a portion of what they are owed or initiate a restructuring. In the majority of cases, however, _____ is initiated by the debtor (a 'voluntary _____' that is filed by the insolvent individual or organization.)
a. 1990 Clean Air Act
b. 33 Strategies of War
c. Bankruptcy
d. 28-hour day

16. _____ is the term used to describe a situation where different entities cooperate advantageously for a final outcome. Simply defined, it means that the whole is greater than the sum of the individual parts. Although the whole will be greater than each individual part, this is not the concept of _____.
a. 1990 Clean Air Act
b. Synergy
c. 33 Strategies of War
d. 28-hour day

17. In economics and especially in the theory of competition, _____ are obstacles in the path of a firm that make it difficult to enter a given market.

_____ are the source of a firm's pricing power - the ability of a firm to raise prices without losing all its customers.

The term refers to hindrances that an individual may face while trying to gain entrance into a profession or trade.

a. Barriers to entry
b. 1990 Clean Air Act
c. Predatory pricing
d. 28-hour day

18. In finance and economics, _____ or divestiture is the reduction of some kind of asset for either financial or ethical objectives or sale of an existing business by a firm. A _____ is the opposite of an investment.

a. 28-hour day
b. 1990 Clean Air Act
c. 33 Strategies of War
d. Divestment

19. _____ are costs that are not directly accountable to a particular function or product. _____ may be either fixed or variable. _____ include taxes, administration, personnel and security costs, and are also known as overhead.
   a. A4e
   b. Indirect costs
   c. A Stake in the Outcome
   d. Activity-based management

20. In economics and related disciplines, a _____ is a cost incurred in making an economic exchange. For example, most people, when buying or selling a stock, must pay a commission to their broker; that commission is a _____ of doing the stock deal. Or consider buying a banana from a store; to purchase the banana, your costs will be not only the price of the banana itself, but also the energy and effort it requires to find out which of the various banana products you prefer, where to get them and at what price, the cost of traveling from your house to the store and back, the time waiting in line, and the effort of the paying itself; the costs above and beyond the cost of the banana are the _____s.
   a. Fixed costs
   b. Cost overrun
   c. Cost accounting
   d. Transaction cost

21. _____ is one of the managerial functions like planning, organizing, staffing and directing. It is an important function because it helps to check the errors and to take the corrective action so that deviation from standards are minimized and stated goals of the organization are achieved in desired manner.According to modern concepts, _____ is a foreseeing action whereas earlier concept of _____ was used only when errors were detected. _____ in management means setting standards, measuring actual performance and taking corrective action.
   a. Decision tree pruning
   b. Control
   c. Schedule of reinforcement
   d. Turnover

22. _____ is, in very basic words, a position a firm occupies against its competitors.

According to Michael Porter, the three methods for creating a sustainable _____ are through:

1. Cost leadership

2. Differentiation

3. Focus (economics)

  a. 28-hour day
  b. Theory Z
  c. 1990 Clean Air Act
  d. Competitive advantage

23. _____, in microeconomics, are the cost advantages that a business obtains due to expansion. They are factors that cause a producer's average cost per unit to fall as scale is increased. _____ is a long run concept and refers to reductions in unit cost as the size of a facility, or scale, increases.
  a. A4e
  b. A Stake in the Outcome
  c. Economies of scale
  d. Economies of scope

24. _____ , also referred to simply as a 'public offering' or 'flotation,' is when a company issues common stock or shares to the public for the first time. They are often issued by smaller, younger companies seeking capital to expand, but can also be done by large privately-owned companies looking to become publicly traded.

In an _____ the issuer may obtain the assistance of an underwriting firm, which helps it determine what type of security to issue (common or preferred), best offering price and time to bring it to market.

  a. Outsourcing
  b. Unemployment insurance
  c. Occupational Safety and Health Administration
  d. Initial public offering

25. _____ is the temporary suspension or permanent termination of employment of an employee or (more commonly) a group of employees for business reasons, such as the decision that certain positions are no longer necessary or a business slow-down or interruption in work. Originally the term '_____' referred exclusively to a temporary interruption in work, as when factory work cyclically falls off. However, in recent times the term can also refer to the permanent elimination of a position.

Chapter 7. Acquisition and Restructuring Strategies

a. Layoff
b. Retirement
c. Termination of employment
d. Wrongful dismissal

26. _____ is the corporate management term for the act of reorganizing the legal, ownership, operational, or other structures of a company for the purpose of making it more profitable, or better organized for its present needs. Alternate reasons for _____ include a change of ownership or ownership structure, demerger repositioning debt _____ and financial _____.
    a. Net worth
    b. Market value added
    c. Market value
    d. Restructuring

27. A _____ is an investment transaction by which an entire company or a controlling part of the stock of a company is sold. A firm 'buys out' a company to take control of it. A _____ can take the form of a leveraged _____, a venture capital _____ or a management _____.
    a. Sweat equity
    b. Shareholder value
    c. Buyout
    d. Gross profit

28. A _____ occurs when a financial sponsor acquires a controlling interest in a company's equity and where a significant percentage of the purchase price is financed through leverage (borrowing.) The assets of the acquired company are used as collateral for the borrowed capital, sometimes with assets of the acquiring company. The bonds or other paper issued for _____ s are commonly considered not to be investment grade because of the significant risks involved.
    a. Limited partners
    b. Growth capital
    c. Venture capital
    d. Leveraged buyout

29. In finance, _____ is an asset class consisting of equity securities in operating companies that are not publicly traded on a stock exchange. Investments in _____ most often involve either an investment of capital into an operating company or the acquisition of an operating company. Capital for _____ is raised primarily from institutional investors.

a. Management buyout
b. Private equity
c. Limited liability company
d. Limited partnership

30. The _____ of 2002 (Pub.L. 107-204, 116 Stat. 745, enacted July 30, 2002), also known as the Public Company Accounting Reform and Investor Protection Act of 2002 and commonly called Sarbanes-Oxley, Sarbox or SOX, is a United States federal law enacted on July 30, 2002, as a reaction to a number of major corporate and accounting scandals including those affecting Enron, Tyco International, Adelphia, Peregrine Systems and WorldCom.
   a. Letter of credit
   b. Fair Labor Standards Act
   c. Sarbanes-Oxley Act
   d. Sarbanes-Oxley Act of 2002

31. In game theory, an _____ is a set of moves or strategies taken by the players, or their payoffs resulting from the actions or strategies taken by all players. The two are complementary in that given knowledge of the set of strategies of all players, the final state of the game is known, as are any relevant payoffs. In a game where chance or a random event is involved, the _____ is not known from only the set of strategies, but is only realized when the random event(s) are realized.
   a. A Stake in the Outcome
   b. A4e
   c. AAAI
   d. Outcome

Chapter 8. International Strategy

1. _____ is exchange of capital, goods, and services across international borders or territories. In most countries, it represents a significant share of gross domestic product (GDP.) While _____ has been present throughout much of history, its economic, social, and political importance has been on the rise in recent centuries.
   a. A4e
   b. A Stake in the Outcome
   c. AAAI
   d. International trade

2. The _____ or gross domestic income (GDI), a basic measure of an economy's economic performance, is the market value of all final goods and services made within the borders of a nation in a year. _____ can be defined in three ways, all of which are conceptually identical. First, it is equal to the total expenditures for all final goods and services produced within the country in a stipulated period of time (usually a 365-day year).
   a. Human capital
   b. Productivity management
   c. Perfect competition
   d. Gross domestic product

3. The _____ is a trilateral trade bloc in North America created by the governments of the United States, Canada, and Mexico. The agreement creating the trade bloc came into force on January 1, 1994. It superseded the Canada-United States Free Trade Agreement between the U.S. and Canada.
   a. Business war game
   b. Trade union
   c. Career portfolios
   d. North American Free Trade Agreement

4. _____ is the branch of economics that studies the dynamics of exchange rates, foreign investment, and how these affect international trade. It also studies international projects, international investments and capital flows, and trade deficits. It includes the study of futures, options and currency swaps.
   a. A4e
   b. AAAI
   c. A Stake in the Outcome
   d. International finance

5. In game theory, an _____ is a set of moves or strategies taken by the players, or their payoffs resulting from the actions or strategies taken by all players. The two are complementary in that given knowledge of the set of strategies of all players, the final state of the game is known, as are any relevant payoffs. In a game where chance or a random event is involved, the _____ is not known from only the set of strategies, but is only realized when the random event(s) are realized.

a. Outcome
b. A Stake in the Outcome
c. AAAI
d. A4e

6. The phrase mergers and _____s refers to the aspect of corporate strategy, corporate finance and management dealing with the buying, selling and combining of different companies that can aid, finance, or help a growing company in a given industry grow rapidly without having to create another business entity.

An _____, also known as a takeover or a buyout, is the buying of one company (the 'target') by another. An _____ may be friendly or hostile.

a. AAAI
b. A4e
c. A Stake in the Outcome
d. Acquisition

7. _____ is, in very basic words, a position a firm occupies against its competitors.

According to Michael Porter, the three methods for creating a sustainable _____ are through:

1. Cost leadership

2. Differentiation

3. Focus (economics)

a. 28-hour day
b. 1990 Clean Air Act
c. Theory Z
d. Competitive advantage

8. In economics and sociology, an _____ is any factor (financial or non-financial) that enables or motivates a particular course of action, or counts as a reason for preferring one choice to the alternatives. It is an expectation that encourages people to behave in a certain way. Since human beings are purposeful creatures, the study of _____ structures is central to the study of all economic activity (both in terms of individual decision-making and in terms of co-operation and competition within a larger institutional structure.)

a. A4e
b. AAAI
c. A Stake in the Outcome
d. Incentive

9. _____ Management is the succession of strategies used by management as a product goes through its _____. The conditions in which a product is sold changes over time and must be managed as it moves through its succession of stages.

The _____ goes through many phases, involves many professional disciplines, and requires many skills, tools and processes.

a. Job hunting
b. Strategic Alliance
c. Golden handshake
d. Product life cycle

10. In economics, _____ is the desire to own something and the ability to pay for it. The term _____ signifies the ability or the willingness to buy a particular commodity at a given point of time.
a. 1990 Clean Air Act
b. 28-hour day
c. 33 Strategies of War
d. Demand

11. In economics and especially in the theory of competition, _____ are obstacles in the path of a firm that make it difficult to enter a given market.

_____ are the source of a firm's pricing power - the ability of a firm to raise prices without losing all its customers.

The term refers to hindrances that an individual may face while trying to gain entrance into a profession or trade.

a. Predatory pricing
b. 1990 Clean Air Act
c. 28-hour day
d. Barriers to entry

12. _____, in microeconomics, are the cost advantages that a business obtains due to expansion. They are factors that cause a producer's average cost per unit to fall as scale is increased. _____ is a long run concept and refers to reductions in unit cost as the size of a facility, or scale, increases.

   a. A4e
   b. Economies of scope
   c. A Stake in the Outcome
   d. Economies of scale

13. _____ is the process of discovering the technological principles of a device, object or system through analysis of its structure, function and operation. It often involves taking something (e.g., a mechanical device, electronic component, or software program) apart and analyzing its workings in detail to be used in maintenance, or to try to make a new device or program that does the same thing without copying anything from the original.

   _____ has its origins in the analysis of hardware for commercial or military advantage .

   a. Predictive maintenance
   b. 28-hour day
   c. Reverse engineering
   d. 1990 Clean Air Act

14. In economics, _____ are the resources employed to produce goods and services. They facilitate production but do not become part of the product (as with raw materials) or significantly transformed by the production process (as with fuel used to power machinery.) To 19th century economists, the _____ were land (natural resources, gifts from nature), labor (the ability to work), and capital goods (human-made tools and equipment.)

   a. Factors of production
   b. Production function
   c. Productive capacity
   d. Multifactor productivity

15. A _____ is a process in which a potential employee is evaluated by an employer for prospective employment in their company, organization and was established in the late 16th century.

   A _____ typically precedes the hiring decision, and is used to evaluate the candidate. The interview is usually preceded by the evaluation of submitted résumés from interested candidates, then selecting a small number of candidates for interviews.

a. Payrolling
b. Supported employment
c. Split shift
d. Job interview

16. A _____ is typically described as a deliberate plan of action to guide decisions and achieve rational outcome(s.) However, the term may also be used to denote what is actually done, even though it is unplanned.

The term may apply to government, private sector organizations and groups, and individuals.

a. Policy
b. 28-hour day
c. 33 Strategies of War
d. 1990 Clean Air Act

17. _____ is the process of dispersing decision-making governance closer to the people or citizen. It includes the dispersal of administration or governance in sectors or areas like engineering, management science, political science, political economy, sociology and economics. _____ is also possible in the dispersal of population and employment.

a. Business plan
b. Formula for Change
c. Frenemy
d. Decentralization

18. _____ as defined in business terms is an organization's strategic guide to globalization. A sound _____ should address these questions: what must be (versus what is) the extent of market presence in the world's major markets? How to build the necessary global presence? What must be (versus what is) the optimal locations around the world for the various value chain activities? How to run global presence into global competitive advantage?

Academic research on _____ came of age during the 1980s, including work by Michael Porter and Christopher Bartlett ' Sumantra Ghoshal. Among the forces perceived to bring about the globalization of competition were convergence in economic systems and technological change, especially in information technology, that facilitated and required the coordination of a multinational firm's strategy on a worldwide scale.

a. 28-hour day
b. 1990 Clean Air Act
c. 33 Strategies of War
d. Global strategy

19. _____, commonly known as e-commerce, consists of the buying and selling of products or services over electronic systems such as the Internet and other computer networks. The amount of trade conducted electronically has grown extraordinarily with widespread Internet usage. The use of commerce is conducted in this way, spurring and drawing on innovations in electronic funds transfer, supply chain management, Internet marketing, online transaction processing, electronic data interchange (EDI), inventory management systems, and automated data collection systems.

   a. A4e
   b. Online shopping
   c. A Stake in the Outcome
   d. Electronic Commerce

20. _____, also referred to simply as a 'public offering' or 'flotation,' is when a company issues common stock or shares to the public for the first time. They are often issued by smaller, younger companies seeking capital to expand, but can also be done by large privately-owned companies looking to become publicly traded.

   In an _____ the issuer may obtain the assistance of an underwriting firm, which helps it determine what type of security to issue (common or preferred), best offering price and time to bring it to market.

   a. Outsourcing
   b. Unemployment insurance
   c. Occupational Safety and Health Administration
   d. Initial public offering

21. The term '_____' refers to the concept of collecting information and attempting to spot a pattern in the information. In some fields of study, the term '_____' has more formally-defined meanings.

   In project management _____ is a mathematical technique that uses historical results to predict future outcome.

   a. Trend analysis
   b. Least squares
   c. Stepwise regression
   d. Regression analysis

22. _____ in its literal sense is the process of transformation of local or regional phenomena into global ones. It can be described as a process by which the people of the world are unified into a single society and function together.

   This process is a combination of economic, technological, sociocultural and political forces.

Chapter 8. International Strategy

a. Collaborative Planning, Forecasting and Replenishment
b. Cost Management
c. Histogram
d. Globalization

23. _____ is a type of trade policy that allows traders to act and transact without interference from government. Thus, the policy permits trading partners mutual gains from trade, with goods and services produced according to the theory of comparative advantage.

Under a _____ policy, prices are a reflection of true supply and demand, and are the sole determinant of resource allocation.

a. 33 Strategies of War
b. 1990 Clean Air Act
c. 28-hour day
d. Free Trade

24. _____ is a designated group of countries that have agreed to eliminate tariffs, quotas and preferences on most (if not all) goods and services traded between them. It can be considered the second stage of economic integration. Countries choose this kind of economic integration form if their economical structures are complementary.

a. 33 Strategies of War
b. 28-hour day
c. 1990 Clean Air Act
d. Free trade area

25. In finance, the _____s between two currencies specifies how much one currency is worth in terms of the other. It is the value of a foreign nation's currency in terms of the home nation's currency. For example an _____ of 102 Japanese yen to the United States dollar means that JPY 102 is worth the same as USD 1.

a. AAAI
b. A4e
c. A Stake in the Outcome
d. Exchange rate

26. A _____ is a business that is privately owned and operated, with a small number of employees and relatively low volume of sales. The legal definition of 'small' often varies by country and industry, but is generally under 100 employees in the United States and under 50 employees in the European Union. In comparison, the definition of mid-sized business by the number of employees is generally under 500 in the U.S. and 250 for the European Union.

a. Critical Success Factor
b. Golden Boot Compensation
c. Pre-determined overhead rate
d. Small business

27.   A _____ is a formal relationship between two or more parties to pursue a set of agreed upon goals or to meet a critical business need while remaining independent organizations.

Partners may provide the _____ with resources such as products, distribution channels, manufacturing capability, project funding, capital equipment, knowledge, expertise, or intellectual property. The alliance is a cooperation or collaboration which aims for a synergy where each partner hopes that the benefits from the alliance will be greater than those from individual efforts.

a. Golden parachute
b. Strategic alliance
c. Process automation
d. Farmshoring

28.   A _____ is an entity formed between two or more parties to undertake economic activity together. The parties agree to create a new entity by both contributing equity, and they then share in the revenues, expenses, and control of the enterprise. The venture can be for one specific project only, or a continuing business relationship such as the Fuji Xerox _____.

a. Civil Rights Act of 1991
b. Patent
c. Joint venture
d. Meritor Savings Bank v. Vinson

29.   An _____ is a person who has possession of an enterprise and assumes significant accountability for the inherent risks and the outcome. It is an ambitious leader who combines land, labor, and capital to create and market new goods or services. The term is a loanword from French and was first defined by the Irish economist Richard Cantillon.

a. A Stake in the Outcome
b. Entrepreneur
c. AAAI
d. A4e

Chapter 8. International Strategy

30. A _____, in business matters, is an entity that is controlled by a bigger and more powerful entity. The controlled entity is called a company, corporation, or limited liability company and in some cases can be a government or state-owned enterprise, and the controlling entity is called its parent (or the parent company.) The reason for this distinction is that a lone company cannot be a _____ of any organization; only an entity representing a legal fiction as a separate entity can be a _____.
   a. 28-hour day
   b. 33 Strategies of War
   c. 1990 Clean Air Act
   d. Subsidiary

31. _____ are legal property rights over creations of the mind, both artistic and commercial, and the corresponding fields of law. Under _____ law, owners are granted certain exclusive rights to a variety of intangible assets, such as musical, literary, and artistic works; ideas, discoveries and inventions; and words, phrases, symbols, and designs. Common types of _____ include copyrights, trademarks, patents, industrial design rights and trade secrets.
   a. Intent
   b. Intellectual property
   c. Equal Pay Act
   d. Unemployment Action Center

32. _____ plant, and equipment, is a term used in accountancy for assets and property which cannot easily be converted into cash. This can be compared with current assets such as cash or bank accounts, which are described as liquid assets. In most cases, only tangible assets are referred to as fixed.
   a. 33 Strategies of War
   b. 28-hour day
   c. 1990 Clean Air Act
   d. Fixed asset

33. In decision theory and estimation theory, the _____ of an estimator, $\hat{\theta}$, of an unknown parameter of the distribution, θ, is the expected value of the loss function

$$R(\theta, \hat{\theta}) = \mathbb{E}_\theta L(\theta, \hat{\theta}) = \int L(\theta, \hat{\theta})\, dP_\theta.$$

where dP_θ is a probability measure parametrized by θ.

- For a scalar parameter θ and a quadratic loss function,

$$L(\theta, \hat{\theta}) = (\theta - \hat{\theta})^2$$

the _____ function becomes the mean squared error of the estimate,

$$R(\theta, \hat{\theta}) = E_\theta (\theta - \hat{\theta})^2$$

- In density estimation, the unknown parameter is probability density itself. The loss function is typically chosen to be a norm in an appropriate function space. For example, for L^2 norm,

$$L(f, \hat{f}) = \|f - \hat{f}\|_2^2$$

the _____ function becomes the mean integrated squared error

$$R(f, \hat{f}) = E\|f - \hat{f}\|^2$$

a. Linear model
b. Risk aversion
c. Financial modeling
d. Risk

34. A _____ is a distinctive sign or indicator used by an individual, business organization, or other legal entity to identify that the products and/or services to consumers with which the _____ appears originate from a unique source and to distinguish its products or services from those of other entities.
    a. Succession planning
    b. Virtual team
    c. Kanban
    d. Trademark

Chapter 9. Cooperative Strategy

1. _____ is an advertisement in which a particular product specifically mentions a competitor by name for the express purpose of showing why the competitor is inferior to the product naming it.

This should not be confused with parody advertisements, where a fictional product is being advertised for the purpose of poking fun at the particular advertisement, nor should it be confused with the use of a coined brand name for the purpose of comparing the product without actually naming an actual competitor. ('Wikipedia tastes better and is less filling than the Encyclopedia Galactica.')

In the 1980s, during what has been referred to as the cola wars, soft-drink manufacturer Pepsi ran a series of advertisements where people, caught on hidden camera, in a blind taste test, chose Pepsi over rival Coca-Cola.

  a. 1990 Clean Air Act
  b. 33 Strategies of War
  c. Comparative advertising
  d. 28-hour day

2. A chief executive officer (_____) or chief executive is one of the highest-ranking corporate officer (executive) or administrator in charge of total management. An individual selected as President and _____ of a corporation, company, organization, or agency, reports to the board of directors. In internal communication and press releases, many companies capitalize the term and those of other high positions, even when they are not proper nouns.
  a. Chief executive officer
  b. Director of communications
  c. Portfolio manager
  d. CEO

3. A _____ is an entity formed between two or more parties to undertake economic activity together. The parties agree to create a new entity by both contributing equity, and they then share in the revenues, expenses, and control of the enterprise. The venture can be for one specific project only, or a continuing business relationship such as the Fuji Xerox _____.
  a. Meritor Savings Bank v. Vinson
  b. Civil Rights Act of 1991
  c. Patent
  d. Joint venture

4. A _____ is a formal relationship between two or more parties to pursue a set of agreed upon goals or to meet a critical business need while remaining independent organizations.

Partners may provide the _____ with resources such as products, distribution channels, manufacturing capability, project funding, capital equipment, knowledge, expertise, or intellectual property. The alliance is a cooperation or collaboration which aims for a synergy where each partner hopes that the benefits from the alliance will be greater than those from individual efforts.

a. Golden parachute
b. Farmshoring
c. Process automation
d. Strategic alliance

5. A _____ is a special kind of database for knowledge management, providing the means for the computerized collection, organization, and retrieval of knowledge.

_____s are categorized into two major types:

- Machine-readable _____s store knowledge in a computer-readable form, usually for the purpose of having automated deductive reasoning applied to them. They contain a set of data, often in the form of rules that describe the knowledge in a logically consistent manner. An ontology can define the structure of stored data - what types of entities are recorded and what their relationships are. Logical operators, such as And (conjunction), Or (disjunction), material implication and negation may be used to build it up from simpler pieces of information. Consequently, classical deduction can be used to reason about the knowledge in the _____. Some machine-readable _____s are used with artificial intelligence, for example as part of an expert system that focuses on a domain like prescription drugs or customs law. Such _____s are also used by the semantic web.

- Human-readable _____s are designed to allow people to retrieve and use the knowledge they contain. They are commonly used to complement a help desk or for sharing information among employees within an organization. They might store troubleshooting information, articles, white papers, user manuals, or answers to frequently asked questions.

a. 1990 Clean Air Act
b. 33 Strategies of War
c. Knowledge base
d. 28-hour day

6. An _____ is a person who has possession of an enterprise and assumes significant accountability for the inherent risks and the outcome. It is an ambitious leader who combines land, labor, and capital to create and market new goods or services. The term is a loanword from French and was first defined by the Irish economist Richard Cantillon.
a. AAAI
b. Entrepreneur
c. A Stake in the Outcome
d. A4e

Chapter 9. Cooperative Strategy

7. _____ is subcontracting a process, such as product design or manufacturing, to a third-party company. The decision to outsource is often made in the interest of lowering cost or making better use of time and energy costs, redirecting or conserving energy directed at the competencies of a particular business, or to make more efficient use of land, labor, capital, (information) technology and resources. _____ became part of the business lexicon during the 1980s.
    a. Unemployment insurance
    b. Operant conditioning
    c. Opinion leadership
    d. Outsourcing

8. _____ is the incidence or process of transferring ownership of a business, enterprise, agency or public service from the public sector (government) to the private sector (business.) In a broader sense, _____ refers to transfer of any government function to the private sector including governmental functions like revenue collection and law enforcement.
    a. Performance reports
    b. 28-hour day
    c. 1990 Clean Air Act
    d. Privatization

9. _____ is a type of private equity capital typically provided to early-stage, high-potential, growth companies in the interest of generating a return through an eventual realization event such as an IPO or trade sale of the company. _____ investments are generally made as cash in exchange for shares in the invested company. It is typical for _____ investors to identify and back companies in high technology industries such as biotechnology and ICT.
    a. Seed round
    b. Private equity
    c. Limited liability corporation
    d. Venture capital

10. _____ refers to the stock of skills and knowledge embodied in the ability to perform labor so as to produce economic value. It is the skills and knowledge gained by a worker through education and experience. Many early economic theories refer to it simply as labor, one of three factors of production, and consider it to be a fungible resource -- homogeneous and easily interchangeable.
    a. Market structure
    b. Human capital
    c. Deflation
    d. Productivity management

11. Price fixing is an agreement between business competitors to sell the same product or service at the same price. In general, it is an agreement intended to ultimately push the price of a product as high as possible, leading to profits for all the sellers. _____ can also involve any agreement to fix, peg, discount or stabilize prices.

Chapter 9. Cooperative Strategy

   a. 33 Strategies of War
   b. 28-hour day
   c. 1990 Clean Air Act
   d. Price-fixing

12. _____ is an agreement, usually secretive, which occurs between two or more persons to deceive, mislead or to obtain an objective forbidden by law typically involving fraud or gaining an unfair advantage. It is an agreement among firms to divide the market, set prices kickbacks, or misrepresenting the independence of the relationship between the colluding parties.' All acts effected by _____ are considered void.
   a. 28-hour day
   b. 1990 Clean Air Act
   c. Collusion
   d. Predatory pricing

13. A _____ is a process in which a potential employee is evaluated by an employer for prospective employment in their company, organization and was established in the late 16th century.

A _____ typically precedes the hiring decision, and is used to evaluate the candidate. The interview is usually preceded by the evaluation of submitted résumés from interested candidates, then selecting a small number of candidates for interviews.

   a. Split shift
   b. Job interview
   c. Supported employment
   d. Payrolling

14. _____ is a legally declared inability or impairment of ability of an individual or organization to pay its creditors. Creditors may file a _____ petition against a debtor ('involuntary _____') in an effort to recoup a portion of what they are owed or initiate a restructuring. In the majority of cases, however, _____ is initiated by the debtor (a 'voluntary _____' that is filed by the insolvent individual or organization.)
   a. 33 Strategies of War
   b. 1990 Clean Air Act
   c. 28-hour day
   d. Bankruptcy

15. _____ is technology based on biology, especially when used in agriculture, food science, and medicine. United Nations Convention on Biological Diversity defines _____ as:

Chapter 9. Cooperative Strategy   87

_____ is often used to refer to genetic engineering technology of the 21st century, however the term encompasses a wider range and history of procedures for modifying biological organisms according to the needs of humanity, going back to the initial modifications of native plants into improved food crops through artificial selection and hybridization. Bioengineering is the science upon which all biotechnological applications are based.

  a. Biotechnology
  b. 33 Strategies of War
  c. 1990 Clean Air Act
  d. 28-hour day

16. The phrase mergers and _____s refers to the aspect of corporate strategy, corporate finance and management dealing with the buying, selling and combining of different companies that can aid, finance, or help a growing company in a given industry grow rapidly without having to create another business entity.

An _____, also known as a takeover or a buyout, is the buying of one company (the 'target') by another. An _____ may be friendly or hostile.

  a. AAAI
  b. A4e
  c. A Stake in the Outcome
  d. Acquisition

17. The _____ or gross domestic income (GDI), a basic measure of an economy's economic performance, is the market value of all final goods and services made within the borders of a nation in a year. _____ can be defined in three ways, all of which are conceptually identical. First, it is equal to the total expenditures for all final goods and services produced within the country in a stipulated period of time (usually a 365-day year).
  a. Gross domestic product
  b. Human capital
  c. Perfect competition
  d. Productivity management

18. _____ are conceptually similar to economies of scale. Whereas economies of scale primarily refer to efficiencies associated with supply-side changes, such as increasing or decreasing the scale of production, of a single product type, _____ refer to efficiencies primarily associated with demand-side changes, such as increasing or decreasing the scope of marketing and distribution, of different types of products. _____ are one of the main reasons for such marketing strategies as product bundling, product lining, and family branding.

Chapter 9. Cooperative Strategy

a. Economies of scale
b. A4e
c. A Stake in the Outcome
d. Economies of scope

19. _____ refers to the methods of practicing and using another person's business philosophy. The franchisor grants the independent operator the right to distribute its products, techniques, and trademarks for a percentage of gross monthly sales and a royalty fee. Various tangibles and intangibles such as national or international advertising, training, and other support services are commonly made available by the franchisor.

a. Franchising
b. 28-hour day
c. 1990 Clean Air Act
d. ServiceMaster

20. _____ is one of the four elements of marketing mix. An organization or set of organizations (go-betweens) involved in the process of making a product or service available for use or consumption by a consumer or business user.

The other three parts of the marketing mix are product, pricing, and promotion.

a. Missing completely at random
b. Matching theory
c. Job creation programs
d. Distribution

21. _____ is an integrated communications-based process through which individuals and communities discover that existing and newly-identified needs and wants may be satisfied by the products and services of others.

_____ is defined by the American _____ Association as the activity, set of institutions, and processes for creating, communicating, delivering, and exchanging offerings that have value for customers, clients, partners, and society at large. The term developed from the original meaning which referred literally to going to market, as in shopping, or going to a market to buy or sell goods or services.

a. Disruptive technology
b. Market development
c. Customer relationship management
d. Marketing

Chapter 9. Cooperative Strategy 89

22. _____ is the state or fact of exclusive rights and control over property, which may be an object, land/real estate or intellectual property. An _____ right is also referred to as title. The concept of _____ has existed for thousands of years and in all cultures.

a. Ownership
b. A4e
c. Emanation of the state
d. A Stake in the Outcome

23. A _____ is typically described as a deliberate plan of action to guide decisions and achieve rational outcome(s.) However, the term may also be used to denote what is actually done, even though it is unplanned.

The term may apply to government, private sector organizations and groups, and individuals.

a. 28-hour day
b. 33 Strategies of War
c. 1990 Clean Air Act
d. Policy

24. In decision theory and estimation theory, the _____ of an estimator, $\hat{\theta}$, of an unknown parameter of the distribution, θ, is the expected value of the loss function

$$R(\theta, \hat{\theta}) = \mathbb{E}_\theta L(\theta, \hat{\theta}) = \int L(\theta, \hat{\theta})\, dP_\theta.$$

where dP_θ is a probability measure parametrized by θ.

- For a scalar parameter θ and a quadratic loss function,

$$L(\theta, \hat{\theta}) = (\theta - \hat{\theta})^2$$

the _____ function becomes the mean squared error of the estimate,

$$R(\theta, \hat{\theta}) = E_\theta(\theta - \hat{\theta})^2$$

- In density estimation, the unknown parameter is probability density itself. The loss function is typically chosen to be a norm in an appropriate function space. For example, for L^2 norm,

$$L(f, \hat{f}) = \|f - \hat{f}\|_2^2$$

the _____ function becomes the mean integrated squared error

$$R(f, \hat{f}) = E\|f - \hat{f}\|^2$$

a. Risk
b. Risk aversion
c. Linear model
d. Financial modeling

25. _____ is a term used in politics and political science. It forms an important rationale as well for transaction cost economics. It is interpreted in different ways, but usually refers to one or more of the following:

- a political style of aiming to increase one's political influence at almost any price, or a political style which involves seizing every and any opportunity to extend one's political influence, whenever such opportunities arise.

- the practice of abandoning in reality some important political principles that were previously held, in the process of trying to increase one's political power and influence.

- a trend of thought, or a political tendency, seeking to make political capital out of situations with the main aim being that of gaining more influence or support, instead of truly winning people over to a principled position or improving their political understanding.

Most politicians are 'opportunists' to some extent at least (they aim to utilize political opportunities to their advantage), but the controversies surrounding the concept concern the exact relationship between 'seizing a political opportunity' and the political principles being espoused.

a. Opportunism
b. AAAI
c. A4e
d. A Stake in the Outcome

26. _____ are legal property rights over creations of the mind, both artistic and commercial, and the corresponding fields of law. Under _____ law, owners are granted certain exclusive rights to a variety of intangible assets, such as musical, literary, and artistic works; ideas, discoveries and inventions; and words, phrases, symbols, and designs. Common types of _____ include copyrights, trademarks, patents, industrial design rights and trade secrets.

a. Intent
b. Intellectual property
c. Unemployment Action Center
d. Equal Pay Act

27. _____ plant, and equipment, is a term used in accountancy for assets and property which cannot easily be converted into cash. This can be compared with current assets such as cash or bank accounts, which are described as liquid assets. In most cases, only tangible assets are referred to as fixed.

a. Fixed asset
b. 33 Strategies of War
c. 28-hour day
d. 1990 Clean Air Act

28. In economics, business, retail, and accounting, a _____ is the value of money that has been used up to produce something, and hence is not available for use anymore. In economics, a _____ is an alternative that is given up as a result of a decision. In business, the _____ may be one of acquisition, in which case the amount of money expended to acquire it is counted as _____.

a. Cost
b. Cost allocation
c. Cost overrun
d. Fixed costs

Chapter 10. Corporate Governance

1. _____ is the set of processes, customs, policies, laws, and institutions affecting the way a corporation (or company) is directed, administered or controlled. _____ also includes the relationships among the many stakeholders involved and the goals for which the corporation is governed. The principal stakeholders are the shareholders/members, management, and the board of directors.
   a. Guarantee
   b. Corporate governance
   c. Flextime
   d. No-FEAR Act

2. A chief executive officer (_____) or chief executive is one of the highest-ranking corporate officer (executive) or administrator in charge of total management. An individual selected as President and _____ of a corporation, company, organization, or agency, reports to the board of directors. In internal communication and press releases, many companies capitalize the term and those of other high positions, even when they are not proper nouns.
   a. Chief executive officer
   b. CEO
   c. Director of communications
   d. Portfolio manager

3. _____ is how top executives of business corporations are paid. This includes a basic salary, bonuses, shares, options and other company benefits. Over the past three decades, _____ has risen dramatically beyond the rising levels of an average worker's wage.
   a. Executive compensation
   b. Association management company
   c. Evidence-based management
   d. Anti-leadership

4. A _____ is a body of elected or appointed members who jointly oversee the activities of a company or organization. The body sometimes has a different name, such as board of trustees, board of governors, board of managers, or executive board. It is often simply referred to as 'the board.'

A board's activities are determined by the powers, duties, and responsibilities delegated to it or conferred on it by an authority outside itself.

   a. Clean Water Act
   b. Competition law
   c. Foreign Corrupt Practices Act
   d. Board of directors

Chapter 10. Corporate Governance

5. A mutual _____ or stockholder is an individual or company (including a corporation) that legally owns one or more shares of stock in a joint stock company. A company's _____s collectively own that company. Thus, the typical goal of such companies is to enhance _____ value.
   a. Stockholder
   b. 1990 Clean Air Act
   c. Free riding
   d. Shareholder

6. _____ is, in very basic words, a position a firm occupies against its competitors.

According to Michael Porter, the three methods for creating a sustainable _____ are through:

1. Cost leadership

2. Differentiation

3. Focus (economics)

   a. 28-hour day
   b. 1990 Clean Air Act
   c. Competitive advantage
   d. Theory Z

7. _____ is one of the managerial functions like planning, organizing, staffing and directing. It is an important function because it helps to check the errors and to take the corrective action so that deviation from standards are minimized and stated goals of the organization are achieved in desired manner. According to modern concepts, _____ is a foreseeing action whereas earlier concept of _____ was used only when errors were detected. _____ in management means setting standards, measuring actual performance and taking corrective action.
   a. Decision tree pruning
   b. Turnover
   c. Schedule of reinforcement
   d. Control

8. A _____ is a process in which a potential employee is evaluated by an employer for prospective employment in their company, organization and was established in the late 16th century.

A _____ typically precedes the hiring decision, and is used to evaluate the candidate. The interview is usually preceded by the evaluation of submitted résumés from interested candidates, then selecting a small number of candidates for interviews.

a. Supported employment
b. Payrolling
c. Split shift
d. Job interview

9. _____ is the state or fact of exclusive rights and control over property, which may be an object, land/real estate or intellectual property. An _____ right is also referred to as title. The concept of _____ has existed for thousands of years and in all cultures.
   a. A Stake in the Outcome
   b. A4e
   c. Emanation of the state
   d. Ownership

10. A _____ is a relatively new executive level position at a corporation, company, organization typically reporting directly to the CEO or board of directors. The _____ is responsible for a brand's image, experience, and promise, and propagating it throughout all aspects of the company. The brand officer oversees marketing, advertising, design, public relations and customer service departments.
    a. Director of communications
    b. Purchasing manager
    c. Chief executive officer
    d. Chief brand officer

11. _____ is a business buzz term, which implies that the ultimate measure of a company's success is to enrich shareholders. It became popular during the 1980s, and is particularly associated with former CEO of General Electric, Jack Welch. In March 2009, Welch openly turned his back on the concept, calling _____ 'the dumbest idea in the world'.
    a. Sweat equity
    b. Shareholder value
    c. Corporate finance
    d. Gross profit margin

12. _____ is a term used in politics and political science. It forms an important rationale as well for transaction cost economics. It is interpreted in different ways, but usually refers to one or more of the following:

- a political style of aiming to increase one's political influence at almost any price, or a political style which involves seizing every and any opportunity to extend one's political influence, whenever such opportunities arise.

- the practice of abandoning in reality some important political principles that were previously held, in the process of trying to increase one's political power and influence.

- a trend of thought, or a political tendency, seeking to make political capital out of situations with the main aim being that of gaining more influence or support, instead of truly winning people over to a principled position or improving their political understanding.

Most politicians are 'opportunists' to some extent at least (they aim to utilize political opportunities to their advantage), but the controversies surrounding the concept concern the exact relationship between 'seizing a political opportunity' and the political principles being espoused.

a. A Stake in the Outcome
b. AAAI
c. A4e
d. Opportunism

13. _____ refers to the movement of cash into or out of a business or financial product. It is usually measured during a specified, finite period of time. Measurement of _____ can be used

- to determine a project's rate of return or value. The time of _____s into and out of projects are used as inputs in financial models such as internal rate of return, and net present value.
- to determine problems with a business's liquidity. Being profitable does not necessarily mean being liquid. A company can fail because of a shortage of cash, even while profitable.
- as an alternate measure of a business's profits when it is believed that accrual accounting concepts do not represent economic realities. For example, a company may be notionally profitable but generating little operational cash (as may be the case for a company that barters its products rather than selling for cash.) In such a case, the company may be deriving additional operating cash by issuing shares evaluating default risk, re-investment requirements, etc.

_____ is a generic term used differently depending on the context. It may be defined by users for their own purposes.

a. Gross profit
b. Gross profit margin
c. Sweat equity
d. Cash flow

Chapter 10. Corporate Governance

14. _____ is a contract between two parties, one being the employer and the other being the employee. An employee may be defined as: 'A person in the service of another under any contract of hire, express or implied, oral or written, where the employer has the power or right to control and direct the employee in the material details of how the work is to be performed.' Black's Law Dictionary page 471 (5th ed. 1979.)
   a. Exit interview
   b. Employment
   c. Employment counsellor
   d. Employment rate

15. In corporate finance, _____ is cash flow available for distribution among all the securities holders of an organization. They include equity holders, debt holders, preferred stock holders, convertible security holders, and so on.

Note that the first three lines above are calculated for you on the standard Statement of Cash Flows.

   a. Kaizen
   b. Pre-determined overhead rate
   c. Policies and procedures
   d. Free cash flow

16. The _____ of an edge is $c_f(u,v) = c(u,v) - f(u,v)$. This defines a residual network denoted $G_f(V, E_f)$, giving the amount of available capacity. See that there can be an edge from u to v in the residual network, even though there is no edge from u to v in the original network.
   a. 33 Strategies of War
   b. 28-hour day
   c. 1990 Clean Air Act
   d. Residual capacity

17. In decision theory and estimation theory, the _____ of an estimator, $\hat{\theta}$, of an unknown parameter of the distribution, θ, is the expected value of the loss function

$$R(\theta, \hat{\theta}) = \mathbb{E}_\theta L(\theta, \hat{\theta}) = \int L(\theta, \hat{\theta})\, dP_\theta.$$

where dP_θ is a probability measure parametrized by θ.

- For a scalar parameter θ and a quadratic loss function,

$$L(\theta, \hat{\theta}) = (\theta - \hat{\theta})^2$$

the _____ function becomes the mean squared error of the estimate,

$$R(\theta, \hat{\theta}) = E_\theta (\theta - \hat{\theta})^2$$

- In density estimation, the unknown parameter is probability density itself. The loss function is typically chosen to be a norm in an appropriate function space. For example, for L^2 norm,

$$L(f, \hat{f}) = \|f - \hat{f}\|_2^2$$

the _____ function becomes the mean integrated squared error

$$R(f, \hat{f}) = E\|f - \hat{f}\|^2$$

a. Risk aversion
b. Financial modeling
c. Linear model
d. Risk

18. An _____ is an economic concept that relates to the cost incurred by an entity (such as organizations) associated with problems such as divergent management-shareholder objectives and information asymmetry. The costs consist of two main sources:

1. The costs inherently associated with using an agent (e.g., the risk that agents will use organizational resource for their own benefit) and
2. The costs of techniques used to mitigate the problems associated with using an agent (e.g., the costs of producing financial statements or the use of stock options to align executive interests to shareholder interests.)

Though effects of _____ are present in any agency relationship, the term is most used in business contexts.

The information asymmetry that exists between shareholders and the Chief Executive Officer is generally considered to be a classic example of a principal-agent problem. The agent (the manager) is working on behalf of the principal (the shareholders), who does not observe the actions of the agent.

a. A4e
b. A Stake in the Outcome
c. AAAI
d. Agency cost

19. In economics, business, retail, and accounting, a _____ is the value of money that has been used up to produce something, and hence is not available for use anymore. In economics, a _____ is an alternative that is given up as a result of a decision. In business, the _____ may be one of acquisition, in which case the amount of money expended to acquire it is counted as _____.

a. Cost
b. Fixed costs
c. Cost allocation
d. Cost overrun

20. In general, a _____ is an arrangement to provide people with an income when they are no longer earning a regular income from employment.

The terms retirement plan or superannuation refer to a _____ granted upon retirement . Retirement plans may be set up by employers, insurance companies, the government or other institutions such as employer associations or trade unions.

a. State Compensation Insurance Fund
b. Pension insurance contract
c. Wage
d. Pension

21. _____ is the point where a person stops employment completely. A person may also semi-retire and keep some sort of _____ job, out of choice rather than necessity. This usually happens upon reaching a determined age, when physical conditions don't allow the person to work any more (by illness or accident), or even for personal choice (usually in the presence of an adequate pension or personal savings.)

a. Severance package
b. Termination of employment
c. Wrongful dismissal
d. Retirement

Chapter 10. Corporate Governance

22. The U.S. _____ is an independent agency of the United States government which holds primary responsibility for enforcing the federal securities laws and regulating the securities industry, the nation's stock and options exchanges, and other electronic securities markets. The SEC was created by section 4 of the Securities Exchange Act of 1934 (now codified as 15 U.S.C. § 78d and commonly referred to as the 1934 Act.)
    a. 1990 Clean Air Act
    b. 28-hour day
    c. 33 Strategies of War
    d. Securities and Exchange Commission

23. _____ in the UK (meaning acquisitions of public companies only) are governed by the City Code on _____ and Mergers, also known as the 'City Code' or 'Takeover Code'. The rules for a takeover, can be found what is primarily known as 'The Blue Book'. The Code used to be a non-statutory set of rules that was controlled by City institutions on a theoretically voluntary basis.
    a. 28-hour day
    b. 33 Strategies of War
    c. 1990 Clean Air Act
    d. Takeovers

24. _____ is a legally declared inability or impairment of ability of an individual or organization to pay its creditors. Creditors may file a _____ petition against a debtor ('involuntary _____') in an effort to recoup a portion of what they are owed or initiate a restructuring. In the majority of cases, however, _____ is initiated by the debtor (a 'voluntary _____' that is filed by the insolvent individual or organization.)
    a. 33 Strategies of War
    b. 1990 Clean Air Act
    c. 28-hour day
    d. Bankruptcy

25. _____ is a civil designation for persons who are incorporated in a fixed or permanent way to a society or group: regular member of the working staff, permanent staff distinguished from a supernumerary.

The term '_____' and its counterpart, 'supernumerary,' originated in Spanish and Latin American academy and government; it is now also used in countries all over the world, such as France, the U.S., England, Italy, etc.

There are _____ members of surgical organizations, of universities, of gastronomical associations, etc.

a. Affiliation
b. Adam Smith
c. Abraham Harold Maslow
d. Numerary

26. The general definition of an _____ is an evaluation of a person, organization, system, process, project or product. _____s are performed to ascertain the validity and reliability of information; also to provide an assessment of a system's internal control. The goal of an _____ is to express an opinion on the person / organization/system (etc) in question, under evaluation based on work done on a test basis.
    a. Audit committee
    b. Audit
    c. A Stake in the Outcome
    d. Internal control

27. In a publicly-held company, an _____ is an operating committee of the Board of Directors, typically charged with oversight of financial reporting and disclosure. Committee members are drawn from members of the Company's board of directors, with a Chairperson selected from among the members. An _____ of a publicly-traded company in the United States is composed of independent and outside directors referred to as non-executive directors, at least one of which is typically a financial expert.
    a. A Stake in the Outcome
    b. Audit committee
    c. Internal auditing
    d. Internal control

28. The _____ of 2002 (Pub.L. 107-204, 116 Stat. 745, enacted July 30, 2002), also known as the Public Company Accounting Reform and Investor Protection Act of 2002 and commonly called Sarbanes-Oxley, Sarbox or SOX, is a United States federal law enacted on July 30, 2002, as a reaction to a number of major corporate and accounting scandals including those affecting Enron, Tyco International, Adelphia, Peregrine Systems and WorldCom.
    a. Sarbanes-Oxley Act
    b. Fair Labor Standards Act
    c. Letter of credit
    d. Sarbanes-Oxley Act of 2002

29. The 'business case for _____', theorizes that in a global marketplace, a company that employs a diverse workforce (both men and women, people of many generations, people from ethnically and racially diverse backgrounds etc.) is better able to understand the demographics of the marketplace it serves and is thus better equipped to thrive in that marketplace than a company that has a more limited range of employee demographics.

Chapter 10. Corporate Governance

An additional corollary suggests that a company that supports the _____ of its workforce can also improve employee satisfaction, productivity and retention.

a. Kanban
b. Trademark
c. Virtual team
d. Diversity

30. _____ are organizations which pool large sums of money and invest those sums in companies. They include banks, insurance companies, retirement or pension funds, hedge funds and mutual funds. Their role in the economy is to act as highly specialized investors on behalf of others.

a. Institutional investors
b. AAAI
c. A Stake in the Outcome
d. A4e

31. An _____ is any party that makes an investment.

The term has taken on a specific meaning in finance to describe the particular types of people and companies that regularly purchase equity or debt securities for financial gain in exchange for funding an expanding company. Less frequently, the term is applied to parties who purchase real estate, currency, commodity derivatives, personal property, or other assets.

a. Investor
b. AAAI
c. A4e
d. A Stake in the Outcome

32. In economics and sociology, an _____ is any factor (financial or non-financial) that enables or motivates a particular course of action, or counts as a reason for preferring one choice to the alternatives. It is an expectation that encourages people to behave in a certain way. Since human beings are purposeful creatures, the study of _____ structures is central to the study of all economic activity (both in terms of individual decision-making and in terms of co-operation and competition within a larger institutional structure.)

a. A Stake in the Outcome
b. Incentive
c. AAAI
d. A4e

33. An _____ is a formal scheme used to promote or encourage specific actions or behavior by a specific group of people during a defined period of time. _____s are particularly used in business management to motivate employees, and in sales in order to attract and retain customers. The scientific literature also refers to this concept as Pay for Performance.
   a. Incentive program
   b. A4e
   c. A Stake in the Outcome
   d. AAAI

34. In finance, an _____ is a contract between a buyer and a seller that gives the buyer the right--but not the obligation-- to buy or to sell a particular asset (the underlying asset) at a later day at an agreed price. In return for granting the _____, the seller collects a payment (the premium) from the buyer. A call _____ gives the buyer the right to buy the underlying asset; a put _____ gives the buyer of the _____ the right to sell the underlying asset.
   a. Option
   b. A4e
   c. A Stake in the Outcome
   d. AAAI

35. The phrase mergers and _____s refers to the aspect of corporate strategy, corporate finance and management dealing with the buying, selling and combining of different companies that can aid, finance, or help a growing company in a given industry grow rapidly without having to create another business entity.

   An _____, also known as a takeover or a buyout, is the buying of one company (the 'target') by another. An _____ may be friendly or hostile.

   a. AAAI
   b. A4e
   c. A Stake in the Outcome
   d. Acquisition

36. A _____ is an agreement between a company and an employee (usually upper executive) specifying that the employee will receive certain significant benefits if employment is terminated. Sometimes, certain conditions, typically a change in company ownership, must be met, but often the cause of termination is unspecified. These benefits may include severance pay, cash bonuses, stock options, or other benefits.
   a. Job hunting
   b. Career development
   c. First-mover advantage
   d. Golden parachute

Chapter 10. Corporate Governance

37. _____, a form of alternative dispute resolution (ADR), is a legal technique for the resolution of disputes outside the courts, wherein the parties to a dispute refer it to one or more persons (the 'arbitrators', 'arbiters' or 'arbitral tribunal'), by whose decision (the 'award') they agree to be bound. It is a settlement technique in which a third party reviews the case and imposes a decision that is legally binding for both sides. Other forms of ADR include mediation (a form of settlement negotiation facilitated by a neutral third party) and non-binding resolution by experts.

    a. AAAI
    b. A Stake in the Outcome
    c. A4e
    d. Arbitration

38. In finance and economics, _____ or divestiture is the reduction of some kind of asset for either financial or ethical objectives or sale of an existing business by a firm. A _____ is the opposite of an investment.

    a. 28-hour day
    b. 1990 Clean Air Act
    c. 33 Strategies of War
    d. Divestment

39. _____ is a term referring to any strategy, generally in business or politics, to increase the likelihood of negative results over positive ones for a party that attempts any kind of takeover. It derives from its original meaning of a literal _____ carried by various spies throughout history, taken when discovered to eliminate the possibility of being interrogated for the enemy's gain.

In publicly held companies, various methods to avoid takeover bids are called '_____s'.

    a. 1990 Clean Air Act
    b. 28-hour day
    c. 33 Strategies of War
    d. Poison pill

40. A _____ is pay and benefits an employee receives when they leave employment at a company. In addition to the employee's remaining regular pay, it may include some of the following:

- An additional payment based on months of service
- Payment for unused vacation time or sick leave.
- A payment in lieu of a required notice period.
- Medical, dental or life insurance
- Retirement (e.g., 401K) benefits
- Stock options
- Assistance in searching for new work, such as access to employment services or help in producing a résumé.

_____s are most typically offered for employees who are laid off or retire. Sometimes, they may be offered for people who resign, regardless of the circumstances; or are fired. Policies for _____s are often found in a company's employee handbook, and in many countries are subject to strict government regulation.

   a. Layoff
   b. Severance package
   c. Retirement
   d. Wrongful dismissal

41. _____ in its literal sense is the process of transformation of local or regional phenomena into global ones. It can be described as a process by which the people of the world are unified into a single society and function together.

This process is a combination of economic, technological, sociocultural and political forces.

   a. Histogram
   b. Collaborative Planning, Forecasting and Replenishment
   c. Globalization
   d. Cost Management

42. A _____ is a set of companies with interlocking business relationships and shareholdings. It is a type of business group.

The prototypical _____ are those which appeared in Japan during the 'economic miracle' following World War II.

   a. 1990 Clean Air Act
   b. 33 Strategies of War
   c. Keiretsu
   d. 28-hour day

Chapter 11. Organizational Structure and Controls

1. An _____ is a mostly hierarchical concept of subordination of entities that collaborate and contribute to serve one common aim.

Organizations are a variant of clustered entities. The structure of an organization is usually set up in many a styles, dependent on their objectives and ambience.

   a. Organizational development
   b. Organizational structure
   c. Open shop
   d. Informal organization

2. _____ is one of the managerial functions like planning, organizing, staffing and directing. It is an important function because it helps to check the errors and to take the corrective action so that deviation from standards are minimized and stated goals of the organization are achieved in desired manner. According to modern concepts, _____ is a foreseeing action whereas earlier concept of _____ was used only when errors were detected. _____ in management means setting standards, measuring actual performance and taking corrective action.
   a. Decision tree pruning
   b. Turnover
   c. Schedule of reinforcement
   d. Control

3. The _____ of 2002 (Pub.L. 107-204, 116 Stat. 745, enacted July 30, 2002), also known as the Public Company Accounting Reform and Investor Protection Act of 2002 and commonly called Sarbanes-Oxley, Sarbox or SOX, is a United States federal law enacted on July 30, 2002, as a reaction to a number of major corporate and accounting scandals including those affecting Enron, Tyco International, Adelphia, Peregrine Systems and WorldCom.
   a. Fair Labor Standards Act
   b. Letter of credit
   c. Sarbanes-Oxley Act of 2002
   d. Sarbanes-Oxley Act

4. _____ is the process by which the activities of an organisation, particularly those regarding decision-making, become concentrated within a particular location and/or group.
   a. Product innovation
   b. Corner office
   c. Centralization
   d. Chief operating officer

Chapter 11. Organizational Structure and Controls

5. In economics, business, retail, and accounting, a _____ is the value of money that has been used up to produce something, and hence is not available for use anymore. In economics, a _____ is an alternative that is given up as a result of a decision. In business, the _____ may be one of acquisition, in which case the amount of money expended to acquire it is counted as _____.
   a. Cost allocation
   b. Fixed costs
   c. Cost overrun
   d. Cost

6. _____ is a concept developed by Michael Porter, used in business strategy. It describes a way to establish the competitive advantage. _____, in basic words, means the lowest cost of operation in the industry.
   a. Strategic group
   b. Switching cost
   c. Strategic business unit
   d. Cost leadership

7. _____ has been described as the 'process of social influence in which one person can enlist the aid and support of others in the accomplishment of a common task' . A definition more inclusive of followers comes from Alan Keith of Genentech who said '_____ is ultimately about creating a way for people to contribute to making something extraordinary happen.'

   _____ is one of the most salient aspects of the organizational context. However, defining _____ has been challenging.

   a. 28-hour day
   b. Situational leadership
   c. Leadership
   d. 1990 Clean Air Act

8. _____ are conceptually similar to economies of scale. Whereas economies of scale primarily refer to efficiencies associated with supply-side changes, such as increasing or decreasing the scale of production, of a single product type, _____ refer to efficiencies primarily associated with demand-side changes, such as increasing or decreasing the scope of marketing and distribution, of different types of products. _____ are one of the main reasons for such marketing strategies as product bundling, product lining, and family branding.
   a. Economies of scope
   b. A4e
   c. A Stake in the Outcome
   d. Economies of scale

Chapter 11. Organizational Structure and Controls

9. _____ is a type of organizational management in which people with similar skills are pooled for work assignments. For example, all engineers may be in one engineering department and report to an engineering manager, but these same engineers may be assigned to different projects and report to a project manager while working on that project. Therefore, each engineer may have to work under several managers to get their job done.
   a. Span of control
   b. Central Administration
   c. Management development
   d. Matrix management

10. _____ is understood as a business unit within the overall corporate identity which is distinguishable from other business because it serves a defined external market where management can conduct strategic planning in relation to products and markets. When companies become really large, they are best thought of as being composed of a number of businesses (or _____s.)

In the broader domain of strategic management, the phrase '_____' came into use in the 1960s, largely as a result of General Electric's many units.

   a. Strategic drift
   b. Strategic group
   c. Switching cost
   d. Strategic business unit

11. _____ as defined in business terms is an organization's strategic guide to globalization. A sound _____ should address these questions: what must be (versus what is) the extent of market presence in the world's major markets? How to build the necessary global presence? What must be (versus what is) the optimal locations around the world for the various value chain activities? How to run global presence into global competitive advantage?

Academic research on _____ came of age during the 1980s, including work by Michael Porter and Christopher Bartlett ' Sumantra Ghoshal. Among the forces perceived to bring about the globalization of competition were convergence in economic systems and technological change, especially in information technology, that facilitated and required the coordination of a multinational firm's strategy on a worldwide scale.

   a. Global strategy
   b. 1990 Clean Air Act
   c. 33 Strategies of War
   d. 28-hour day

12. A _____ is a process in which a potential employee is evaluated by an employer for prospective employment in their company, organization and was established in the late 16th century.

108 *Chapter 11. Organizational Structure and Controls*

A _____ typically precedes the hiring decision, and is used to evaluate the candidate. The interview is usually preceded by the evaluation of submitted résumés from interested candidates, then selecting a small number of candidates for interviews.

  a. Supported employment
  b. Payrolling
  c. Split shift
  d. Job interview

13. _____ is subcontracting a process, such as product design or manufacturing, to a third-party company. The decision to outsource is often made in the interest of lowering cost or making better use of time and energy costs, redirecting or conserving energy directed at the competencies of a particular business, or to make more efficient use of land, labor, capital, (information) technology and resources. _____ became part of the business lexicon during the 1980s.
  a. Opinion leadership
  b. Outsourcing
  c. Unemployment insurance
  d. Operant conditioning

14. _____ refers to the methods of practicing and using another person's business philosophy. The franchisor grants the independent operator the right to distribute its products, techniques, and trademarks for a percentage of gross monthly sales and a royalty fee. Various tangibles and intangibles such as national or international advertising, training, and other support services are commonly made available by the franchisor.
  a. ServiceMaster
  b. 28-hour day
  c. Franchising
  d. 1990 Clean Air Act

15. A _____ is a formal relationship between two or more parties to pursue a set of agreed upon goals or to meet a critical business need while remaining independent organizations.

Partners may provide the _____ with resources such as products, distribution channels, manufacturing capability, project funding, capital equipment, knowledge, expertise, or intellectual property. The alliance is a cooperation or collaboration which aims for a synergy where each partner hopes that the benefits from the alliance will be greater than those from individual efforts.

a. Golden parachute
b. Strategic alliance
c. Process automation
d. Farmshoring

16. _____ is, in very basic words, a position a firm occupies against its competitors.

According to Michael Porter, the three methods for creating a sustainable _____ are through:

1. Cost leadership

2. Differentiation

3. Focus (economics)

a. Theory Z
b. Competitive advantage
c. 1990 Clean Air Act
d. 28-hour day

Chapter 12. Strategic Leadership

1. _____ has been described as the 'process of social influence in which one person can enlist the aid and support of others in the accomplishment of a common task'. A definition more inclusive of followers comes from Alan Keith of Genentech who said '_____ is ultimately about creating a way for people to contribute to making something extraordinary happen.'

_____ is one of the most salient aspects of the organizational context. However, defining _____ has been challenging.

   a. Situational leadership
   b. 1990 Clean Air Act
   c. 28-hour day
   d. Leadership

2. A chief executive officer (_____) or chief executive is one of the highest-ranking corporate officer (executive) or administrator in charge of total management. An individual selected as President and _____ of a corporation, company, organization, or agency, reports to the board of directors. In internal communication and press releases, many companies capitalize the term and those of other high positions, even when they are not proper nouns.
   a. CEO
   b. Chief executive officer
   c. Portfolio manager
   d. Director of communications

3. A _____ is a body of elected or appointed members who jointly oversee the activities of a company or organization. The body sometimes has a different name, such as board of trustees, board of governors, board of managers, or executive board. It is often simply referred to as 'the board.'

A board's activities are determined by the powers, duties, and responsibilities delegated to it or conferred on it by an authority outside itself.

   a. Competition law
   b. Foreign Corrupt Practices Act
   c. Board of directors
   d. Clean Water Act

4. _____ is a process of planning and controlling the performance or execution of any type of activity, such as:

   - a project (project _____) or
   - a process (process _____, sometimes referred to as the process performance measurement and management system.)

Organization's senior management is responsible for carrying out its _____.

a. Participatory management
b. Work design
c. Human Relations Movement
d. Management process

5. _____ refers to the stock of skills and knowledge embodied in the ability to perform labor so as to produce economic value. It is the skills and knowledge gained by a worker through education and experience. Many early economic theories refer to it simply as labor, one of three factors of production, and consider it to be a fungible resource -- homogeneous and easily interchangeable.
   a. Market structure
   b. Human capital
   c. Deflation
   d. Productivity management

6. The term _____ collectively refers to all resources that determine the value and the competitiveness of an enterprise. As such, it includes as subsets the attributes that concur to building all financial statements as well as the balance sheet.
   a. A4e
   b. Intellectual capital
   c. A Stake in the Outcome
   d. AAAI

7. _____ is, in very basic words, a position a firm occupies against its competitors.

According to Michael Porter, the three methods for creating a sustainable _____ are through:

1. Cost leadership

2. Differentiation

3. Focus (economics)

   a. Theory Z
   b. 1990 Clean Air Act
   c. 28-hour day
   d. Competitive advantage

8. A _____ is directly responsible for managing the day-to-day operations (and profitability) of a company.

Chief Executive Officer (CEO)
- As the top manager, the CEO is typically responsible for the entire operations of the corporation and reports directly to the chairman and board of directors. It is the CEO's responsibility to implement board decisions and initiatives and to maintain the smooth operation of the firm, with the assistance of senior management.

   a. Field service management
   b. Getting Things Done
   c. Management team
   d. Vorstand

9.   A _____ is a process in which a potential employee is evaluated by an employer for prospective employment in their company, organization and was established in the late 16th century.

A _____ typically precedes the hiring decision, and is used to evaluate the candidate. The interview is usually preceded by the evaluation of submitted résumés from interested candidates, then selecting a small number of candidates for interviews.

   a. Payrolling
   b. Split shift
   c. Job interview
   d. Supported employment

10.   In economics, the people in the _____ are the suppliers of labor. The _____ is all the nonmilitary people who are employed or unemployed. In 2005, the worldwide _____ was over 3 billion people.
   a. Decent work
   b. Pink-collar worker
   c. Departmentalization
   d. Labor force

11.   A _____ is a special kind of database for knowledge management, providing the means for the computerized collection, organization, and retrieval of knowledge.

Chapter 12. Strategic Leadership

_____s are categorized into two major types:

- Machine-readable _____s store knowledge in a computer-readable form, usually for the purpose of having automated deductive reasoning applied to them. They contain a set of data, often in the form of rules that describe the knowledge in a logically consistent manner. An ontology can define the structure of stored data - what types of entities are recorded and what their relationships are. Logical operators, such as And (conjunction), Or (disjunction), material implication and negation may be used to build it up from simpler pieces of information. Consequently, classical deduction can be used to reason about the knowledge in the _____. Some machine-readable _____s are used with artificial intelligence, for example as part of an expert system that focuses on a domain like prescription drugs or customs law. Such _____s are also used by the semantic web.

- Human-readable _____s are designed to allow people to retrieve and use the knowledge they contain. They are commonly used to complement a help desk or for sharing information among employees within an organization. They might store troubleshooting information, articles, white papers, user manuals, or answers to frequently asked questions.

a. Knowledge base
b. 1990 Clean Air Act
c. 33 Strategies of War
d. 28-hour day

12. A _____ is a compensation, usually financial, received by a worker in exchange for their labor.

Compensation in terms of _____s is given to worker and compensation in terms of salary is given to employees. Compensation is a monetary benefits given to employees in returns of the services provided by them.

a. Profit-sharing agreement
b. Wage
c. Performance-related pay
d. State Compensation Insurance Fund

13. Income disparity or _____ is a term used to describe inequities and asymmetry in the distribution of wealth and income between socio-economic groups within society. The term also has many other definitions:

Common examples include:

- The income gap between the wealthy and the poor.
- lower average income for females than males

In the context of economic inequality, gender gap generally refers to the differences in the wages of men and women, or boys and girls. There is a debate to what extent this is the result of gender differences, lifestyle choices (e.g., number of hours worked), or because of discrimination.

A United Nations report found that women working in manufacturing earned the following percentages in relation to men in 2003.

   a. Workforce
   b. Quality of working life
   c. Wage gap
   d. Division of labour

14. The _____ is the labour pool in employment. It is generally used to describe those working for a single company or industry, but can also apply to a geographic region like a city, country, state, etc. The term generally excludes the employers or management, and implies those involved in manual labour.
   a. Division of labour
   b. Work-life balance
   c. Pink-collar worker
   d. Workforce

15. _____ is an organization's process of defining its strategy and making decisions on allocating its resources to pursue this strategy, including its capital and people. Various business analysis techniques can be used in _____, including SWOT analysis (Strengths, Weaknesses, Opportunities, and Threats) and PEST analysis (Political, Economic, Social, and Technological analysis) or STEER analysis involving Socio-cultural, Technological, Economic, Ecological, and Regulatory factors and EPISTEL (Environment, Political, Informatic, Social, Technological, Economic and Legal)

_____ is the formal consideration of an organization's future course. All _____ deals with at least one of three key questions:

   1. 'What do we do?'
   2. 'For whom do we do it?'
   3. 'How do we excel?'

In business _____, the third question is better phrased 'How can we beat or avoid competition?'. (Bradford and Duncan, page 1.)

Chapter 12. Strategic Leadership

a. 28-hour day
b. Strategic planning
c. 1990 Clean Air Act
d. 33 Strategies of War

16. The _____ is a trilateral trade bloc in North America created by the governments of the United States, Canada, and Mexico. The agreement creating the trade bloc came into force on January 1, 1994. It superseded the Canada-United States Free Trade Agreement between the U.S. and Canada.
   a. Business war game
   b. Career portfolios
   c. Trade union
   d. North American Free Trade Agreement

17. _____ is something that a firm can do well and that meets the following three conditions:

Competencies are things that companys execute well across several business units or product sectors.

Firms usually have few competencies, but these are usually less liable to change rapidly.

   1. It provides consumer benefits
   2. It is not easy for competitors to imitate
   3. It can be leveraged widely to many products and markets.

A _____ can take various forms, including technical/subject matter know-how, a reliable process and/or close relationships with customers and suppliers (Mascarenhas et al. 1998.)

   a. Dominant Design
   b. Learning-by-doing
   c. NAIRU
   d. Core competency

18. An _____ is a person who has possession of an enterprise and assumes significant accountability for the inherent risks and the outcome. It is an ambitious leader who combines land, labor, and capital to create and market new goods or services. The term is a loanword from French and was first defined by the Irish economist Richard Cantillon.
   a. AAAI
   b. A4e
   c. Entrepreneur
   d. A Stake in the Outcome

19. _____ is a type of private equity capital typically provided to early-stage, high-potential, growth companies in the interest of generating a return through an eventual realization event such as an IPO or trade sale of the company. _____ investments are generally made as cash in exchange for shares in the invested company. It is typical for _____ investors to identify and back companies in high technology industries such as biotechnology and ICT.

   a. Seed round
   b. Limited liability corporation
   c. Private equity
   d. Venture capital

20. _____ is the temporary suspension or permanent termination of employment of an employee or (more commonly) a group of employees for business reasons, such as the decision that certain positions are no longer necessary or a business slow-down or interruption in work. Originally the term '_____' referred exclusively to a temporary interruption in work, as when factory work cyclically falls off. However, in recent times the term can also refer to the permanent elimination of a position.

   a. Retirement
   b. Termination of employment
   c. Layoff
   d. Wrongful dismissal

21. In the field of human resource management, _____ is the field concerned with organizational activity aimed at bettering the performance of individuals and groups in organizational settings. It has been known by several names, including employee development, human resource development, and learning and development.

Harrison observes that the name was endlessly debated by the Chartered Institute of Personnel and Development during its review of professional standards in 1999/2000.

   a. Performance appraisal
   b. Revolving door syndrome
   c. Training and development
   d. Person specification

22. _____ is an idea in the field of Organizational studies and management which describes the psychology, attitudes, experiences, beliefs and Values (personal and cultural values) of an organization. It has been defined as 'the specific collection of values and norms that are shared by people and groups in an organization and that control the way they interact with each other and with stakeholders outside the organization.'

Chapter 12. Strategic Leadership 117

This definition continues to explain organizational values also known as 'beliefs and ideas about what kinds of goals members of an organization should pursue and ideas about the appropriate kinds or standards of behavior organizational members should use to achieve these goals. From organizational values develop organizational norms, guidelines or expectations that prescribe appropriate kinds of behavior by employees in particular situations and control the behavior of organizational members towards one another.'

_____ is not the same as corporate culture.

a. Organizational development
b. Organizational effectiveness
c. Organizational culture
d. Union shop

23. A _____ is a set of companies with interlocking business relationships and shareholdings. It is a type of business group.

The prototypical _____ are those which appeared in Japan during the 'economic miracle' following World War II.

a. 33 Strategies of War
b. 28-hour day
c. 1990 Clean Air Act
d. Keiretsu

24. In decision theory and estimation theory, the _____ of an estimator, $\hat{\theta}$, of an unknown parameter of the distribution, θ, is the expected value of the loss function

$$R(\theta, \hat{\theta}) = \mathbb{E}_\theta L(\theta, \hat{\theta}) = \int L(\theta, \hat{\theta})\, dP_\theta.$$

where dP_θ is a probability measure parametrized by θ.

- For a scalar parameter θ and a quadratic loss function,

$$L(\theta, \hat{\theta}) = (\theta - \hat{\theta})^2$$

the _____ function becomes the mean squared error of the estimate,

$$R(\theta, \hat{\theta}) = E_\theta(\theta - \hat{\theta})^2$$

- In density estimation, the unknown parameter is probability density itself. The loss function is typically chosen to be a norm in an appropriate function space. For example, for L^2 norm,

$$L(f, \hat{f}) = \|f - \hat{f}\|_2^2$$

the _____ function becomes the mean integrated squared error

$$R(f, \hat{f}) = E\|f - \hat{f}\|^2$$

a. Risk aversion
b. Financial modeling
c. Linear model
d. Risk

25. The _____ of 2002 (Pub.L. 107-204, 116 Stat. 745, enacted July 30, 2002), also known as the Public Company Accounting Reform and Investor Protection Act of 2002 and commonly called Sarbanes-Oxley, Sarbox or SOX, is a United States federal law enacted on July 30, 2002, as a reaction to a number of major corporate and accounting scandals including those affecting Enron, Tyco International, Adelphia, Peregrine Systems and WorldCom.
a. Fair Labor Standards Act
b. Sarbanes-Oxley Act
c. Letter of credit
d. Sarbanes-Oxley Act of 2002

26. The U.S. _____ is an independent agency of the United States government which holds primary responsibility for enforcing the federal securities laws and regulating the securities industry, the nation's stock and options exchanges, and other electronic securities markets. The SEC was created by section 4 of the Securities Exchange Act of 1934 (now codified as 15 U.S.C. § 78d and commonly referred to as the 1934 Act.)

a. Securities and Exchange Commission
b. 1990 Clean Air Act
c. 28-hour day
d. 33 Strategies of War

27. A _____ is a set of rules outlining the responsibilities of or proper practices for an individual or organization. Related concepts include ethical codes and honor codes.

In its 2007 International Good Practice Guidance, Defining and Developing an Effective _____ for Organizations, the International Federation of Accountants provided the following working definition:

'Principles, values, standards, or rules of behavior that guide the decisions, procedures and systems of an organization in a way that (a) contributes to the welfare of its key stakeholders, and (b) respects the rights of all constituents affected by its operations.'

a. 28-hour day
b. Code of conduct
c. 1990 Clean Air Act
d. 33 Strategies of War

28. _____ is a term used in politics and political science. It forms an important rationale as well for transaction cost economics. It is interpreted in different ways, but usually refers to one or more of the following:

- a political style of aiming to increase one's political influence at almost any price, or a political style which involves seizing every and any opportunity to extend one's political influence, whenever such opportunities arise.

- the practice of abandoning in reality some important political principles that were previously held, in the process of trying to increase one's political power and influence.

- a trend of thought, or a political tendency, seeking to make political capital out of situations with the main aim being that of gaining more influence or support, instead of truly winning people over to a principled position or improving their political understanding.

Most politicians are 'opportunists' to some extent at least (they aim to utilize political opportunities to their advantage), but the controversies surrounding the concept concern the exact relationship between 'seizing a political opportunity' and the political principles being espoused.

a. AAAI
b. A4e
c. A Stake in the Outcome
d. Opportunism

29. The _____ is a performance management tool for measuring whether the smaller-scale operational activities of a company are aligned with its larger-scale objectives in terms of vision and strategy.

By focusing not only on financial outcomes but also on the operational, marketing and developmental inputs to these, the _____ helps provide a more comprehensive view of a business, which in turn helps organizations act in their best long-term interests. This tool is also being used to address business response to climate change and greenhouse gas emissions.

a. Commercial management
b. Middle management
c. Balanced scorecard
d. Management development

30. _____ is one of the managerial functions like planning, organizing, staffing and directing. It is an important function because it helps to check the errors and to take the corrective action so that deviation from standards are minimized and stated goals of the organization are achieved in desired manner. According to modern concepts, _____ is a foreseeing action whereas earlier concept of _____ was used only when errors were detected. _____ in management means setting standards, measuring actual performance and taking corrective action.

a. Decision tree pruning
b. Schedule of reinforcement
c. Turnover
d. Control

31. A _____ or business method is a collection of related, structured activities or tasks that produce a specific service or product (serve a particular goal) for a particular customer or customers. It often can be visualized with a flowchart as a sequence of activities.

There are three types of _____ es:

1. Management processes, the processes that govern the operation of a system. Typical management processes include 'Corporate Governance' and 'Strategic Management'.
2. Operational processes, processes that constitute the core business and create the primary value stream. Typical operational processes are Purchasing, Manufacturing, Marketing, and Sales.
3. Supporting processes, which support the core processes. Examples include Accounting, Recruitment, Technical support.

A _____ begins with a customer's need and ends with a customer's need fulfillment. Process oriented organizations break down the barriers of structural departments and try to avoid functional silos.

a. 1990 Clean Air Act
b. 28-hour day
c. 33 Strategies of War
d. Business process

32. The _____ or gross domestic income (GDI), a basic measure of an economy's economic performance, is the market value of all final goods and services made within the borders of a nation in a year. _____ can be defined in three ways, all of which are conceptually identical. First, it is equal to the total expenditures for all final goods and services produced within the country in a stipulated period of time (usually a 365-day year).

a. Productivity management
b. Perfect competition
c. Gross domestic product
d. Human capital

33. The phrase mergers and _____ s refers to the aspect of corporate strategy, corporate finance and management dealing with the buying, selling and combining of different companies that can aid, finance, or help a growing company in a given industry grow rapidly without having to create another business entity.

An _____, also known as a takeover or a buyout, is the buying of one company (the 'target') by another. An _____ may be friendly or hostile.

a. AAAI
b. Acquisition
c. A4e
d. A Stake in the Outcome

Chapter 13. Strategic Entrepreneurship

1. _____ according to Onuoha (2007) is the practice of starting new organizations or revitalizing mature organizations, particularly new businesses generally in response to identified opportunities. _____ is often a difficult undertaking, as a vast majority of new businesses fail. Entrepreneurial activities are substantially different depending on the type of organization that is being started.
    a. AAAI
    b. Entrepreneurship
    c. A Stake in the Outcome
    d. A4e

2. An _____ is a person who has possession of an enterprise and assumes significant accountability for the inherent risks and the outcome. It is an ambitious leader who combines land, labor, and capital to create and market new goods or services. The term is a loanword from French and was first defined by the Irish economist Richard Cantillon.
    a. A4e
    b. A Stake in the Outcome
    c. Entrepreneur
    d. AAAI

3. A _____ is a set of exclusive rights granted by a state to an inventor or his assignee for a limited period of time in exchange for a disclosure of an invention.

    The procedure for granting _____s, the requirements placed on the _____ee and the extent of the exclusive rights vary widely between countries according to national laws and international agreements. Typically, however, a _____ application must include one or more claims defining the invention which must be new, inventive, and useful or industrially applicable.

    a. Labor Management Reporting and Disclosure Act
    b. Federal Trade Commission Act
    c. Patent
    d. Food, Drug, and Cosmetic Act

4. A chief executive officer (_____) or chief executive is one of the highest-ranking corporate officer (executive) or administrator in charge of total management. An individual selected as President and _____ of a corporation, company, organization, or agency, reports to the board of directors. In internal communication and press releases, many companies capitalize the term and those of other high positions, even when they are not proper nouns.
    a. CEO
    b. Portfolio manager
    c. Chief executive officer
    d. Director of communications

Chapter 13. Strategic Entrepreneurship

5. _____ is a term used to describe any moral, political that stresses human interdependence and the importance of a collective, rather than the importance of separate individuals. Collectivists focus on community and society, and seek to give priority to group goals over individual goals. The philosophical underpinnings of _____ are for some related to holism or organicism - the view that the whole is greater than the sum of its parts/pieces.
   a. Collectivism
   b. 28-hour day
   c. Collaborative methods
   d. 1990 Clean Air Act

6. _____ refers to the stock of skills and knowledge embodied in the ability to perform labor so as to produce economic value. It is the skills and knowledge gained by a worker through education and experience. Many early economic theories refer to it simply as labor, one of three factors of production, and consider it to be a fungible resource -- homogeneous and easily interchangeable.
   a. Productivity management
   b. Market structure
   c. Human capital
   d. Deflation

7. The term _____ collectively refers to all resources that determine the value and the competitiveness of an enterprise. As such, it includes as subsets the attributes that concur to building all financial statements as well as the balance sheet.
   a. A4e
   b. A Stake in the Outcome
   c. Intellectual capital
   d. AAAI

8. A _____ is a special kind of database for knowledge management, providing the means for the computerized collection, organization, and retrieval of knowledge.

_____s are categorized into two major types:

- Machine-readable _____s store knowledge in a computer-readable form, usually for the purpose of having automated deductive reasoning applied to them. They contain a set of data, often in the form of rules that describe the knowledge in a logically consistent manner. An ontology can define the structure of stored data - what types of entities are recorded and what their relationships are. Logical operators, such as And (conjunction), Or (disjunction), material implication and negation may be used to build it up from simpler pieces of information. Consequently, classical deduction can be used to reason about the knowledge in the _____. Some machine-readable _____s are used with artificial intelligence, for example as part of an expert system that focuses on a domain like prescription drugs or customs law. Such _____s are also used by the semantic web.

- Human-readable _____s are designed to allow people to retrieve and use the knowledge they contain. They are commonly used to complement a help desk or for sharing information among employees within an organization. They might store troubleshooting information, articles, white papers, user manuals, or answers to frequently asked questions.

a. 33 Strategies of War
b. 28-hour day
c. 1990 Clean Air Act
d. Knowledge base

9. In business and engineering, new _____ is the term used to describe the complete process of bringing a new product or service to market. There are two parallel paths involved in the NProduct development process: one involves the idea generation, product design, and detail engineering; the other involves market research and marketing analysis. Companies typically see new _____ as the first stage in generating and commercializing new products within the overall strategic process of product life cycle management used to maintain or grow their market share.
a. 33 Strategies of War
b. Product development
c. 1990 Clean Air Act
d. 28-hour day

10. _____ is technology based on biology, especially when used in agriculture, food science, and medicine. United Nations Convention on Biological Diversity defines _____ as:

_____ is often used to refer to genetic engineering technology of the 21st century, however the term encompasses a wider range and history of procedures for modifying biological organisms according to the needs of humanity, going back to the initial modifications of native plants into improved food crops through artificial selection and hybridization. Bioengineering is the science upon which all biotechnological applications are based.

a. 28-hour day
b. 1990 Clean Air Act
c. 33 Strategies of War
d. Biotechnology

11. The phrase mergers and _____s refers to the aspect of corporate strategy, corporate finance and management dealing with the buying, selling and combining of different companies that can aid, finance, or help a growing company in a given industry grow rapidly without having to create another business entity.

An _____, also known as a takeover or a buyout, is the buying of one company (the 'target') by another. An _____ may be friendly or hostile.

a. A Stake in the Outcome
b. A4e
c. AAAI
d. Acquisition

12. A _____ is a process in which a potential employee is evaluated by an employer for prospective employment in their company, organization and was established in the late 16th century.

A _____ typically precedes the hiring decision, and is used to evaluate the candidate. The interview is usually preceded by the evaluation of submitted résumés from interested candidates, then selecting a small number of candidates for interviews.

a. Split shift
b. Job interview
c. Supported employment
d. Payrolling

13. A _____ is a subset of the overall internal controls of a business covering the application of people, documents, technologies, and procedures by management accountants to solving business problems such as costing a product, service or a business-wide strategy. _____s are distinct from regular information systems in that they are used to analyze other information systems applied in operational activities in the organization. Academically, the term is commonly used to refer to the group of information management methods tied to the automation or support of human decision making, e.g. Decision Support Systems, Expert systems, and Executive information systems.

a. Management Information system
b. 28-hour day
c. Strategic information system
d. 1990 Clean Air Act

14. _____ is a type of private equity capital typically provided to early-stage, high-potential, growth companies in the interest of generating a return through an eventual realization event such as an IPO or trade sale of the company. _____ investments are generally made as cash in exchange for shares in the invested company. It is typical for _____ investors to identify and back companies in high technology industries such as biotechnology and ICT.

a. Venture capital
b. Seed round
c. Private equity
d. Limited liability corporation

15. The _____ is an agency of the United States Department of Health and Human Services and is responsible for regulating and supervising the safety of foods, dietary supplements, drugs, vaccines, biological medical products, blood products, medical devices, radiation-emitting devices, veterinary products, and cosmetics. The FDA also enforces section 361 of the Public Health Service Act and the associated regulations, including sanitation requirements on interstate travel as well as specific rules for control of disease on products ranging from pet turtles to semen donations for assisted reproductive medicine techniques.

The FDA is an agency within the United States Department of Health and Human Services responsible for protecting and promoting the nation's public health.

a. 28-hour day
b. 1990 Clean Air Act
c. 33 Strategies of War
d. Food and Drug Administration

ANSWER KEY

Chapter 1
1. c 2. a 3. a 4. a 5. a 6. a 7. b 8. a 9. d 10. a
11. c 12. d 13. c 14. b 15. d 16. c 17. d 18. d 19. d 20. a
21. d 22. b 23. a 24. d 25. c 26. d 27. a 28. d 29. b 30. a
31. c 32. c 33. d 34. d

Chapter 2
1. d 2. d 3. c 4. d 5. a 6. d 7. a 8. c 9. c 10. c
11. a 12. d 13. c 14. d 15. d 16. c 17. d 18. a 19. d 20. d
21. c 22. d 23. d 24. d 25. a 26. a 27. a 28. d 29. c 30. b
31. d 32. a 33. d 34. d 35. d 36. b 37. c 38. d 39. d 40. d
41. a 42. d 43. c 44. d 45. b 46. b 47. c 48. a 49. d

Chapter 3
1. c 2. d 3. d 4. d 5. d 6. d 7. b 8. d 9. d 10. d
11. c 12. a 13. d 14. d 15. b 16. d 17. b 18. c 19. d 20. d
21. d 22. d 23. c 24. a 25. d 26. c 27. d

Chapter 4
1. a 2. b 3. d 4. a 5. c 6. d 7. c 8. d 9. d 10. d
11. c 12. d 13. d 14. d 15. d 16. a 17. d 18. d 19. a 20. d
21. b 22. c 23. c 24. d 25. d 26. b 27. d 28. d

Chapter 5
1. b 2. d 3. d 4. c 5. d 6. d 7. b 8. d 9. b 10. d
11. d 12. d 13. d

Chapter 6
1. d 2. a 3. d 4. d 5. d 6. d 7. c 8. d 9. d 10. d
11. d 12. c 13. a 14. c 15. b 16. d 17. d 18. d 19. d 20. d
21. d 22. d 23. d 24. a 25. c 26. d 27. d 28. b 29. d 30. c
31. d 32. a 33. c 34. d 35. c 36. b 37. d 38. d 39. d

Chapter 7
1. a 2. d 3. d 4. d 5. d 6. d 7. c 8. a 9. d 10. d
11. d 12. a 13. d 14. a 15. c 16. b 17. a 18. d 19. b 20. d
21. b 22. d 23. c 24. d 25. a 26. d 27. c 28. d 29. b 30. c
31. d

Chapter 8
1. d 2. d 3. d 4. d 5. a 6. d 7. d 8. d 9. d 10. d
11. d 12. d 13. c 14. a 15. d 16. a 17. d 18. d 19. d 20. d
21. a 22. d 23. d 24. d 25. d 26. d 27. b 28. c 29. b 30. d
31. b 32. d 33. d 34. d

Chapter 9

1. c	2. d	3. d	4. d	5. c	6. b	7. d	8. d	9. d	10. b
11. d	12. c	13. b	14. d	15. a	16. d	17. a	18. d	19. a	20. d
21. d	22. a	23. d	24. a	25. a	26. b	27. a	28. a		

Chapter 10

1. b	2. b	3. a	4. d	5. d	6. c	7. d	8. d	9. d	10. d
11. b	12. d	13. d	14. b	15. d	16. d	17. d	18. d	19. a	20. d
21. d	22. d	23. d	24. d	25. d	26. b	27. b	28. a	29. d	30. a
31. a	32. b	33. a	34. a	35. d	36. d	37. d	38. d	39. d	40. b
41. c	42. c								

Chapter 11

1. b	2. d	3. d	4. c	5. d	6. d	7. c	8. a	9. d	10. d
11. a	12. d	13. b	14. c	15. b	16. b				

Chapter 12

1. d	2. a	3. c	4. d	5. b	6. b	7. d	8. c	9. c	10. d
11. a	12. b	13. c	14. d	15. b	16. d	17. d	18. c	19. d	20. c
21. c	22. c	23. d	24. d	25. b	26. a	27. b	28. d	29. c	30. d
31. d	32. c	33. b							

Chapter 13

1. b	2. c	3. c	4. a	5. a	6. c	7. c	8. d	9. b	10. d
11. d	12. b	13. a	14. a	15. d					

www.ingramcontent.com/pod-product-compliance
Lightning Source LLC
Chambersburg PA
CBHW082046230426

43670CB00016B/2797